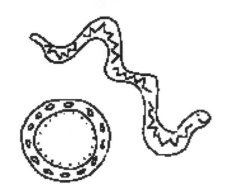

Movement Stories
For Young Children
Ages 3–6

Smith and Kraus *Books For Actors*
YOUNG ACTORS SERIES

If you require pre-publication information about upcoming Smith and Kraus books, you may receive our annual catalogue, free of charge, by sending your name and address to *Smith and Kraus Catalogue, P.O. Box 127, One Main Street, Lyme, NH 03768, call us at (888) 282-2881, fax (603) 643-1831, or visit www.smithandkraus.com.*

Movement Stories

For Young Children
Ages 3–6

by Helen Landalf and Pamela Gerke

Young Actors Series

SK
A Smith and Kraus Book

A Smith and Kraus Book
Published by Smith and Kraus, Inc.
One Main Street, PO Box 127, Lyme, NH 03768

First Edition: September 1996
9 8 7 6 5 4 3 2 1

Library of Congress Cataloging-in-Publication Date

Landalf, Helen.
Movement stories for young children ages 3–6 / by Helen Landalf and Pamela Gerke.
p. cm. —(Young actors series)
Includes bibliographical references.
ISBN 1-57525-048-9
1. Movement education. 2. Storytelling. I. Gerke, Pamela. II. Title. III. Series.
GV425.L34 1996
372.86—dc20 96-26754
CIP

ACKNOWLEDGEMENTS

Thank you to all the teachers who helped test these stories in their classes. Ruth Bachrach, Lynn Beasley, Janie Cantwell, Fran Dearmin, Pam Myers, Marilyn Ostrom, and Alina Rossano.

Thank you to all the children who helped test these stories at: Apollo Elementary Preschool & Head Start Program, Creative Dance Center, 55th Street School, Magnolia Presbyterian Church, and Wallingford Cooperative Preschool.

Thank you to Daniel Johnson, Krista Harris and Bette Lamont for providing information on Laban Movement Analysis and Developmental Movement.

Thank you to Anne Green Gilbert and the faculty of Creative Dance Center, Michael Clawsen, and Eric Johnson for ideas and inspiration.

Thank you to Marisa Smith, Eric Kraus, Julia Hill, and the staff at Smith and Kraus, Inc. for their help and support in creating this book.

DEDICATION

This book is dedicated to Anne Green Gilbert
in gratitude for many years of encouragement and inspiration.

CONTENTS

• • •

Why Movement?

. . .

WHY MOVEMENT?

Movement is the currency of life. Even when our bodies are at rest there is movement in the slow rise and fall of our breath and the coursing of blood through our veins. We move to survive, to learn, to discover where we end and the outer world begins.

Young children, in particular, have a nearly insatiable desire for movement. Witness the desperate striving of a toddler to take his or her first step, the breathless, active bodies of children on a playground, or the constant squirming of students confined to desks, and you will see how powerful the drive toward movement can be.

But, all too soon, we expect children to suppress the urge to move—to sit still, be quiet, stop fidgeting, pay attention. Many educational systems, in particular, seem to operate from the viewpoint that unless children are sitting still, solemnly facing the teacher, they are not learning.

Fortunately, educational researchers are beginning to discover that nothing could be further from the truth. With the publication of *Frames of Mind,* Howard Gardner's groundbreaking work on the Multiple Intelligences, new interest is being focused on the "kinesthetic learner"—the child who actually learns best through movement.

Not only kinesthetic learners, but all students can derive numerous benefits from the use of movement as an educational tool. Body awareness, coordination, flexibility, and spatial awareness are some of the physical skills a child gains through movement. A child's cognitive skills develop through vocabulary building and creative problem solving, while his or her social/emotional self grows through cooperation with others and a growing sense of self-esteem. The very functioning of the brain itself is enhanced through the repetition of specific developmental movements. Movement truly fosters the development of the whole child: body, mind, and spirit.

•

MOVEMENT AND THE BRAIN

From earliest infancy, our bodies strive to interact with the world. As we lie on our backs, we squirm and move our limbs. On our tummies, we press our arms into the floor, lifting our heads in an effort to see our surroundings. Soon we "crawl," pulling ourselves along the floor on our bellies. Later we "creep," moving more efficiently on our hands and knees. Finally, we are walking—taking huge strides toward the things we desire.

What may seem to be a purely physical progression is actually much more complicated. Each stage in our development of mobility corresponds to the development of an area in our brains. Our brains cannot develop properly without movement—the two are inextricably linked. Movement affects our ability to see, hear, feel, use our hands, understand and use language, and even our ability to read, think, and organize information.

In fact, research has shown that children who do not, for some reason, go through each stage of this natural movement progression are very likely to experience impaired brain functioning. Because impairments at a lower level also disrupt functioning at higher levels of the brain, this dysfunction may manifest as a learning disability, attention deficit, or any number of debilitating disorders. So, in fact, we can actually disable a child by not allowing him or her to move.

There is a great deal of evidence that such disorders can be treated by encouraging the child to reexperience the developmental phase that he or she missed. By repeating the movements natural to that stage of development, the brain has a renewed opportunity to form the neurological pathways we need for optimal mental and physical performance.

One significant change in movement patterning that happens during early childhood is the transition from homolateral (one-sided) to cross-lateral (two-sided) movement. In homolateral movement, one side of the body moves as a unit. When babies are first learning to crawl, they move forward with the arm and leg on one side of the body, then switch to the other side. Gradually, the body begins to learn a way to move more efficiently. The right arm and left leg begin to move simultaneously, followed by a step with the left arm and right leg. This is cross-lateral movement—the movement pattern used by most humans throughout their lives.

Aside from helping the child move more efficiently through the world, cross-lateral movement also serves a deeper purpose—it develops nerve fibers that connect the two hemispheres of the brain. It also encourages the eyes to track from side to side, which is an essential prereading skill. Children who have difficulty with cross-lateral movement very often show evidence of learning disabilities, particularly reading problems.

Another skill that children develop naturally through movement is spatial orientation, the ability to know where one is in space, which is connected to balance. Children who have difficulty with balance can often be helped through the practice of vestibular stimulation, which simply involves spinning, turning, swinging, or rocking as a means of shaking up the fluid in the inner ear. It is the movement of this fluid that helps us balance and orient ourselves in space.

The role of movement in developing a healthy, fully functioning brain would seem to be reason enough to include it as a part of each child's education. However, movement provides numerous other benefits as well. Movement experiences also positively affect the physical, intellectual, emotional, and social development of a child.

•

MOVEMENT AND THE MIND

The kinds of experiences that the Movement Stories in this book provide engage both the creative and logical aspects of the mind. The imaginativeness of the stories motivates children to listen, concentrate, and follow directions—essential skills for any learning situation. As Movement Concepts are introduced and explored, the child is building vocabulary which relates not only to movement but to daily living. In addition, because the directions in most of the stories allow for more than one correct response, the stories also contain many opportunities for problem-solving. For example, in the story "The Painter and the Elves," children will use creative problem solving to discover how many different ways they can paint the floor with their bodies!

As you share Movement Stories with your students, you may notice several students who seem to "take" to movement more than others. (They may also be the students who have difficulty focusing when asked to sit still and listen.) These students could be kinesthetic learners: those who receive information primarily through movement and touch. It is very important to provide movement experiences daily in your classroom in order to reach these learners. You will also find that many of your students will retain information more easily if you teach it through movement. This is because movement involves children in learning actively, rather than just listening passively.

Many of the stories in this book can be adapted to enhance learning in other areas of your curriculum (see the Extension section at the end of each story). You will also find a multitude of ideas for integrating movement into your classroom in Anne Green Gilbert's *Teaching the 3 Rs Through Movement Experiences* (see Bibliography).

·

MOVEMENT AND THE BODY

It should be quite obvious that movement experiences can benefit the physical development of a child. A well-rounded movement program helps children develop body awareness, strength, and flexibility, as well as balance and coordination. The child who has the opportunity for movement on a consistent basis improves his or her gross motor skills, develops strong, flexible muscles, and increases stamina. In addition, movement provides an opportunity for the release of pent-up energy and sends blood flowing throughout the system, increasing oxygen to the brain. The physical release of moving can help a child concentrate more easily on academic subjects.

In our age of television and computers, it is particularly important that children begin to enjoy and value movement at an early age. Young children who experience the joy and pleasure of moving creatively are more likely to make physical expression a part of their lives and less likely to incur the health risks of a sedentary lifestyle.

·

MOVEMENT AND THE EMOTIONS

In contrast to the "sports" approach to physical education, which tends to treat movement as purely functional, the experiences in this book will lead a child toward using movement as a form of self-expression, thus involving his or her emotions. The stories encourage children to explore and create their own movements within a structure, rather than asking them to simply imitate the teacher, thus removing anxiety about doing something the "right" way. Because many varying responses can be correct, children are encouraged to grow in their sense of self-esteem. Movement Stories take movement out of the competitive field and into the personal, expressive realm.

Children's responses to these stories will be highly personal. In asking students to move on a low level, for example, some students will choose to move quickly, some slowly, some forward, some backward, some smoothly, some sharply. Their choices will reflect their personal preferences, as well as how they are feeling at that particular moment. By giving them the opportunity to express the uniqueness of their spirits in movement, you will be opening a powerful new avenue for self-expression in their lives.

Many of the Movement Concepts deal with contrasts (High–Low, Big–Little, Strong–Light, Smooth–Sharp, and so on), giving children who explore these concepts experiences of moving in ways that are unfamiliar and even in direct opposition to their habitual ways of interacting with the world. This serves to broaden the child's image of his or her self, making available alternate choices for self-expression. For example, a child who usually moves very lightly and delicately may, through experiencing the concept of Weight (Heavy and Light), suddenly perceive that he or she can also be very strong and powerful. Experiencing these contrasts can also increase a child's sense of empathy with those who move through life differently than him or herself.

In addition to increasing a child's self-awareness (what Howard Gardner calls the "intrapersonal intelligence"), movement can also help children develop positive interactions with others (the "interpersonal intelligence"). Children moving to these stories will experience sharing space with others and learn to value individual differences by observing other students' movement responses. Moving as a group also encourages a class or group of children to bond with each other and to bond with you as a teacher.

•

WHY MOVEMENT STORIES?

Though movement can certainly be taught through a competitive approach ("Let's see who is the fastest runner") or a "drill" approach ("Let's all gallop around the room three times"), most children will respond more readily and consistently to movement experiences that speak to their creativity and sense of imagination. Shy or inhibited children, in particular, often feel safer moving as a character in a story than simply moving as themselves.

Because the Movement Stories in this book are based on concepts that are introduced at the beginning of each story, children are being provided with a broad vocabulary and a conceptual framework for understanding movement. The child who understands these concepts will be able to use them in many situations outside of the Movement Stories themselves. For example, children who have experienced the concept of Self-space, and know that they have a personal kinesphere that needs to grow or shrink to accommodate the kinespheres of others, will have an easier time finding an empty spot in a crowded lunchroom. Children who have learned the concept Pathways and have physically experienced the difference between a straight and a curved line will more readily be able to form letters on a page. The child who has experienced the contrast between strong and light Weight and knows how to withhold some of his or her strength in order to move delicately will truly know what it means to handle an object gently. These are but a few examples of the numerous ways in which the Movement Concepts interface with everyday life.

Finally, it is important to realize that Movement Stories are only a beginning. We encourage all teachers to make a conceptually based movement program, of which these Movement Stories can be an integral part, a weekly or biweekly event in their classrooms. For advice on how to plan an entire lesson based on a Movement Concept, see "Planning a Complete Movement Lesson" in Chapter 3, "How to Use This Book." *Creative Dance for All Ages* by Anne Green Gilbert is also a highly recommended source on planning a complete movement program. (See Bibliography.)

We hope that you will find sharing Movement Stories with your students to be a richly rewarding experience. Enjoy!

Movement Concepts

• • •

BODY

Body Parts: Head, Arms, Elbows, Hands, Back, Stomach, Legs, Feet, and so on

Body Shape: Straight, Curved, Angular, Twisted, Wide, Narrow

Balance: On Balance, Off Balance

SPACE

Place: Self-space, General Space

Level: High, Middle, Low

Direction: Forward, Backward, Right, Left, Up, Down

Pathway: Straight, Curved, Zigzag

Size: Big, Medium, Little

Relationship: Over, Under, Around, Through, Together, Apart, and so on

QUALITY

Speed: Slow, Medium, Fast

Rhythm: Pulse, Breath, Pattern

Weight :   Strong, Light

Energy: Smooth, Sharp

Flow: Free, Bound

Focus: Single focus, Multifocus

A Partial Listing of Locomotor and Nonlocomotor Movements

• • •

Locomotor (traveling)	Nonlocomotor (stationary)
crawl	bend
gallop	carve
hop	dab
jump	flick
leap	float
roll	glide
run	poke
scoot	press
slide	punch
slither	shake
tiptoe	slash
walk	spin
	squirm
	stretch
	swing
	turn
	twist
	wiggle
	wring

Using this chart: The words on this chart can be called out as suggestions during any free dance period in a story or lesson. For example, if children are exploring moving in different directions, encourage them with suggestions like: "Has anyone tried jumping backward? How about shaking forward? Could you float sideways?" These words will help students vary the kinds of movements they choose to do, instead of always walking or running.

It is highly recommended that you make a large copy of both this chart and the Movement Concepts chart for your classroom wall, so that you can refer to them easily while teaching.

What are Movement Concepts?

· · ·

The basic Movement Concepts discussed in this book were originally defined and recorded by Rudolph von Laban in the 1930s in his attempt to describe and analyze movement and to establish a notation system for movement similar to the one used to notate music. These concepts underlie all movements, whether they be dance steps, athletic feats, pedestrian movements, or even the movements of animals or machines.

Over the years many variations of Laban's vocabulary have evolved and many movement educators, ourselves included, no longer adhere strictly to his original terminology. In this book we use vocabulary similar to that developed by Anne Green Gilbert, an internationally recognized dance educator and founder of the Creative Dance Center in Seattle, Washington. Though our organization of the concepts is slightly different from Gilbert's, it is similar enough to make this book compatible with her highly recommended materials. (See Bibliography.) For the purposes of this book we will divide the concepts into the following three areas:

1. Body—including the Parts of the body that can move and the Shapes that the body can take.

2. Space—where the body moves in space, including the Level, Direction, Pathway, and Size of a movement.

3. Quality—whether the movement is slow or fast, strong or light, smooth or sharp, and so forth.

The following section contains a short description of each Movement Concept, followed by a simple idea for exploring the concept with young children. You may want to read the entire section once to acquaint yourself with all of the concepts. It is also suggested that you refresh your memory by reviewing the applicable concept(s) before telling a Movement Story. This will facilitate your ability to present the story clearly to your students. For a complete listing of the concepts, see the Movement Concepts chart at the beginning of this chapter.

·

BODY

All of the concepts in the area of Body define how the body itself moves, exclusive of the body's relationship to space, time, or other people. Since the body is our tool or instrument, this area of movement is of primary importance. For young children who are just discovering their own unique physical selves, it is an essential concept to explore.

Body Parts:

Head, Neck, Shoulders, Spine, Arms, Elbows, Hands, Stomach, Hips, Legs, Feet, and so forth.

The body can be divided into many different parts which can be moved in isolation (i.e. standing still while only moving your head), in combination (i.e. moving elbows and knees simultaneously), or moving all parts together as one unit. Body parts can lead us through space, move us along the floor, and help us create shapes.

Idea for Exploring: Have students stand in one place. Call out the name of a body part (i.e. "elbows"). When the music plays, students will move only that part. When the music stops, they stop their movement and listen for the next body part to be called.

Shapes:

Straight, Curved, Angular, Twisted, Wide, Narrow, Symmetrical, Asymmetrical

Our bodies can make shapes. If we stretch all of our body parts, a straight shape is created. When we bend our joints we are making an angular shape. Softening or rotating our body parts creates shapes that are curved or twisted. Shapes can also be wide, narrow, symmetrical (the same on both sides), or asymmetrical (different on each side).

Shapes can remain stationary, like a still photograph in one spot, or they can move through space. It is also possible for us to change shapes while we are moving. We can make shapes alone or with other dancers.

Idea for Exploring: As you shake a tambourine, students move freely around the room (or you can direct their movement, asking them to gallop, jump, move backward, and so forth). When you hit the tambourine, students create shapes with their bodies. Alternate between moving and creating shapes.

Balance:

On, Off

When our body is on balance, as when we're standing with two feet planted firmly on the floor, we feel stable and connected to the ground. When our body is off balance, as when we lean or tip, we feel as if we might fall. The challenge is to go off balance but still be in control.

We can make many kinds of balancing shapes: balancing on one foot, on a hand and a foot, on a bottom, and so on. We can also go off balance as we move by tipping, swirling or spinning on one leg.

Idea for Exploring: Encourage students to experiment with the many types of balancing shapes they can create. Call out specific body parts for them to place on the floor (i.e. "Balance on one foot…two hands and one foot…your stomach…your back"). Or, simply call out a number and let them place that number of body parts on the floor, independently choosing which body parts to use. For example: If you call out the number "three," some students will balance on two feet and one hand, others on two hands and one foot, others on two elbows and one knee, and so forth.

•

SPACE

The concept area of Space defines the expanse we are moving through and how we get from one place to another. The same principles of Space apply whether we are moving in a large gymnasium or in a small corner of a classroom. The more children understand about their relationship to space, the more orderly and less confusing the physical world will seem to them.

Place:

Self-space, General Space

The concept of Place tells us whether we are moving on one spot (Self-space) or traveling through space (General Space). Movement done in place is called nonlocomotor movement while traveling steps are known as locomotor movements. (See chart of Locomotor and Nonlocomotor Movements at the beginning of this chapter.) Whether we travel or stay in one place, we have a personal space or "kinesphere" which serves as a boundary between our own space and the space of others. Our kinesphere is like a giant bubble that surrounds our body. It can expand or shrink, depending on how much space is available to move in and how close to others we feel comfortable being in any given situation.

Children who are exposed to the concept of Place will find it easier to move in the vicinity of others without bumping or crashing. By giving them the option to move in one spot and encouraging them to find empty spaces as they visualize their own kinesphere and the kinespheres of others, they become more aware of their placement in the room and more responsible in their relationships to other movers.

Idea for Exploring: Have students alternate moving in one place with dancing freely around the room. You may want to call out various nonlocomotor movements for them to try in Self-space and locomotor movements for them to do in General Space. (See Locomotor and Nonlocomotor Movement chart.) It's also fun to dance in self- and General Space with props, such as scarves or crepe paper streamers.

Size:
Big, Medium, Little

As we move in Self- or General Space, we can vary the amount of area our movement takes up. Big movements reach far into space, with the body parts stretching far apart, while little movements stay very close to the center of the body. We change the size of a shape or movement by growing or shrinking. It is important to note that "big" is not synonymous with "tall"—it is possible to make a big shape by lying on the floor with our body parts stretched far apart. We can, in the same way, remain standing and be "little" by holding our body parts close together.

Children who naturally do very big movements, often unintentionally knocking things over or hurting others, can learn to be more careful by being given an opportunity to practice small movements. Children who are shy or timid may find it easier to be more confident and assertive if they have a chance to practice large movements. It is also helpful to practice growing and shrinking, fluctuating between big and small.

Idea for Exploring: Alternately playing soft and loud sounds, have students try movements that are very tiny and very big. You can use music that changes in volume or play two different instruments, such as a drum (for big movements) and a triangle (for little movements). Children relate well to images such as moving like elves (small) and giants (big).

Directions:
Forward, Backward, Right, Left, Up, Down

We can move through General Space in any of the six directions listed above. Direction is determined by the surface of the body that is leading us through space: The front of the body leads us forward, the back of our body leads us backward, the sides of our body lead us right and left, the top of our body leads us up, and the bottom of our body leads us down.

It is important to differentiate "direction" from "facing," which is determined by a place in the room. For example, you might be facing a window, moving forward toward it, but you could also turn your back to the window and move backward toward it. You could also turn, face another side of the room, and move forward to another direction.

Idea for Exploring: Play music and call out a direction, i.e., "backward." Children move in that direction till the music stops. Call out a new direction for each change in the music. It's fun to pretend that the children are being pulled by "magic magnets."

Levels:

Low, Middle, High

Level determines whether we are close to the ground or far away. Low-level movement is very close to the floor. Slithering, creeping (on hands and knees), and rolling are common low-level movements. In high-level movement the body is at its full height or in the air. Walking on tiptoe, skipping, and leaping are examples of high-level movement. Middle-level movement is movement in between low and high. Some examples of middle level movement are walking crouched over, walking on one's knees with the body upright, or "crab-walking" (hands and feet on the floor, stomach toward the ceiling).

We can also change levels as we move. Rising is the action of changing from low level to high and sinking is the action of changing from high level to low.

Idea for Exploring: Have children think of animals that move on each level. They could be snakes and lizards moving on a low level, crabs, cats and elephants moving on a middle level, and people, giraffes and birds moving on a high level. Do this with background music playing, calling out one level at a time and letting them freely explore animal movements on that level.

Pathways:

Straight, Curved, Zigzag

Pathways are the designs our body parts create as they move through space and the designs our feet make as we move across the floor. You might think of your pathway as the "jet stream" you leave behind as you move. When you move in straight pathways you are moving only in straight lines and turning corners sharply. Curved pathways can take the form of circles, spirals, or waves. Zigzag pathways are straight pathways that change direction sharply, as in the contours of lightning or mountain ranges. Pathways can be created on the floor with the feet (or other body parts if moving at a low or middle level) or in the air by moving arms, heads, elbows, and so on.

Idea for Exploring: Have students take an imaginary trip using different pathways. They could drive an imaginary car in a straight pathway, fly an airplane in curved pathways, and hike up a mountain in zigzag pathways. Allow them to brainstorm other forms of transportation and the kinds of pathways they would create.

Relationships:

Near, Far, Over, Under, Around, Through, Above, Below, On, Off, and so forth.

As we move, we are creating relationships between our body parts. We might be moving with all of our body parts near each other, with our arms overhead, or with our hands on our hips. In addition, we may choose to create relationships with objects (a chair, a scarf, a balloon) or with other people. Sometimes all three types of relationships may be happening at once!

Relationships can happen in stillness and in movement. For example, you might make a still shape over a scarf or skip around a partner. When having relationships with other movers, we can relate to one other person (a partner) or a group of people. It is possible for partners or groups to move over, under, around, and through each other. Moving in relationship to others requires awareness and cooperation, essential elements in building social skills.

Idea for Exploring: Have students explore creating relationships with a scarf. Encourage them to move under the scarf, jump over the scarf, tiptoe around the scarf, roll on the scarf, and balance the scarf on one of their body parts. After they have explored individual relationships with the scarf, guide them in coming together as a group, moving their scarves in the center of the group like a fountain, then dancing apart.

•

QUALITY

The concept area of Quality defines how a movement is performed: slowly or quickly, strongly or lightly, smoothly, or sharply, and so on. Movement researcher Rudolph von Laban called this area of movement "Effort" because of the varying degrees of energy required to complete specific types of movements. The quality of a movement is affected by the inner image our mind holds while moving (i.e., "lightly as a feather"). Quality can also be affected by an attitude or feeling (i.e., feeling luxurious when moving slowly, feeling urgent when moving quickly).

Speed:
> Slow, Medium, Fast

The Speed or tempo at which your body moves determines how much time it takes you to complete a movement. Some movements tend to be done slowly, such as floating, melting, and stretching. Other movements are usually done at a fast speed: running, shaking, spinning. A large number of movements can be done at any speed. For example: walking, turning, and twisting could each be done very slowly, extremely quickly, or at any speed in between. Each of these movements could also accelerate (get faster and faster) or decelerate (become progressively slower).

Many children tend to move quite quickly and find it a challenge to slow down. For this reason, moving at a variety of speeds is important to practice often.

Idea for Exploring: Have students alternate between moving slowly and moving quickly. When moving slowly, ask them to imagine that they are just waking up—yawning, stretching, rolling slowly out of bed, and so on. When moving quickly, encourage them to imagine that they are in a big hurry. Support this exploration by playing two different selections of music, one fast and one slow, or a piece of music that alternates between slow and fast.

Rhythm:
> Pulse, Breath, Pattern

Rhythm is the pattern our movements make in time. The rhythm of our movement can be an even pulse, like a heartbeat, or free flowing and varied, like our breath. When we divide time into beats of different lengths we create a rhythmic pattern.

Most young children have an innate sense of rhythm, but don't necessarily enjoy analyzing it in an intellectual way. At this age, it is best to allow them to learn by doing—moving their bodies freely to music with different rhythms or playing musical instruments as they practice keeping a steady beat. Rhythmic songs and chants are another excellent tool for developing a sense of rhythm.

Idea for Exploring: Play different types of music (i.e., a march, a waltz, a polka) and allow children to move freely while playing musical instruments. Encourage movements that reflect the rhythm of the music (i.e., marching, turning, galloping).

Weight:

Strong, Light

The quality of Weight defines how we are using our muscles as we move—either with strength and power or lightly and delicately. There are two ways of moving with strong weight. When we use strong weight actively we contract out muscles and press, pull, punch, or slash. When we use strong weight passively our muscles are limp and our bodies are heavy, giving in to the pull of gravity. Light movement requires withholding part of one's weight to produce a delicate, lifted feeling. Examples of light movement are floating, flicking, dabbing, and scampering. However, many movements can be done either strongly or lightly.

Idea for Exploring: Ask students to name some things that move lightly, i.e., a cloud floating, a cotton ball rolling, a mouse scampering. Next, ask them to name some things that move strongly, i.e., a weight lifter, an elephant, a karate master. Then have them show their ideas in movement, moving lightly when soft or delicate music is played and strongly when loud or powerful music is played. You could also accompany them with two different musical instruments (see the Idea for Exploring the concept of Size).

Energy:

Smooth, Sharp

When our Energy is smooth, our movement is ongoing, without stops. Another name for this is "sustained" movement. In contrast, sharp movement is full of quick stops. It can also be called "percussive" or "sudden" movement.

Imagery is often helpful in evoking smooth or sharp movement. Some images for smooth movement might be: painting a wall, clouds floating, birds gliding through the air. Some images for sharp movement might be: punching an enemy, popping a balloon, swatting a fly.

Idea for Exploring: Using balloons, have the students alternate between smooth and sharp movement. They could float, swirl, turn, and roll with their balloons smoothly, then bat, tap, and kick them sharply. After repeating this exploration several times, challenge them to try it without the balloons! Music with clear legato and staccato sections works well for this exploration.

Flow:

Free, Bound

When we move with free flow we move with abandon, allowing the movement to flow through our bodies without trying to control or stop it. This might have the sensation of wind or water moving through our bodies and is very smooth and ongoing. Bound flow, by contrast, is very controlled. This could take the form of jerky, robot-like movement or movement with extreme caution or control, as in walking a tightrope. Flow, like all movement qualities, exists on a continuum—absolutely free, moderately free, slightly free to slightly bound, moderately bound, extremely bound.

Some of your students (or yourself!) may tend to move through life in a free-flowing way—"going with the flow" with very little preplanning, and perhaps being physically reckless. These students can benefit greatly by practicing bound flow movement.

On the other hand, you may also have students who seem very cautious and controlled, afraid to take any risks. These students can open up a great deal through experiencing free-flowing movement. Experiencing the continuum—gradating from one extreme to the other—is helpful for both types of people.

Idea for Exploring: Have students move freely, imagining that a wind is blowing them around the room or that they are a flowing river. Contrast this with moving like robots or machines, keeping their bodies very controlled.

Focus:

Single Focus, Multifocus

Focus defines how we direct our attention as we move. When we use single focus, all of our attention is directed toward one thing at a time. We may simply look at one object, place, or, person or we may reach toward it or move toward it. We can change our point of focus very rapidly but as long as we focus on one thing at a time we are using single focus.

When we allow our attention to widen we are using multifocus. This is when we direct our attention toward many things at once. We might imagine that we are scanning a horizon. Our eyes look at many places in the room and our body might be turning or weaving in space.

Idea for Exploring: Call out different points of focus as students move around the room (i.e., "focus on your hand," "focus on the ceiling," "focus on your toe," "focus on a friend"). It helps to play music during the movement then stop it between each focus task to give children a chance to stop and redirect their attention.

A final note: Though each concept has been described here separately, the Movement Concepts never function in isolation. Even in the act of walking across the room, you will be using several different concepts at once: You may be walking in a forward Direction at a high Level and a fast Speed through general Space! The combining of Movement Concepts is what makes the possibilities of movement infinitely creative and exciting.

How To Use This Book

• • •

WHAT MOVEMENT STORIES ARE

Movement Stories are tales told for the purpose of introducing and exploring Movement Concepts. The stories in this book are written with a thorough understanding of movement education for children and are designed to elicit specific movements that will enhance child development. At the same time, these stories are calculated to appeal to a child's sense of fun and imagination so that children will be fully interested and engaged in the activity. One definition of "fun" is that our human system is designed so as to make us want to do that which is good for our own development. Movement Stories are fun for children! The stories in this book and others like them satisfy both the imagination and developmental needs of children.

Movement Stories are not the same as creative dramatics. While dramatics, like Movement Stories, are fun and serve child-development needs, these activities teach about plot, setting, character, voice projection, stage presence, and other theater arts skills—subjects that are not specifically addressed in Movement Stories. Movement Stories differ from creative dramatics in that they are primarily designed to advance kinesthetic learning and self-expression through movement education principles; whereas creative dramatics promote learning via theater arts (for more on dramatics for children, see *Multicultural Plays for Children, Grades K–6* by Pamela Gerke and other publications by Smith & Kraus, Inc.).

•

WHO CAN USE MOVEMENT STORIES

Movement Stories appeal to children of all ages because they involve imagination, fun and physical action. Although the stories in this book were designed for ages 3–6, they have, in fact, been proven successful with children up to age twelve! These stories can be used in preschool, kindergarten, and first-grade classrooms, as well as day care centers, before- and after-school childcare classes, play groups, and by parents and other adults who work with children. Movement Stories work well with children of all abilities and have been proven successful with children with learning disabilities, physical restrictions, and other special needs.

•

WHEN TO USE MOVEMENT STORIES

Movement Stories are useful and appropriate in a variety of classroom situations. Movement Stories are great for transition times between activities because they immediately engage the attention of all the children and bring the group together. Likewise, they are excellent activities for the beginning or the ending of the school day. On rainy days, when "cabin fever" is running high, Movement Stories provide a welcome outlet for physical energy indoors. Movement Stories can be used in physical education classes as well.

Movement Stories make school subjects come alive! Integrating movement into the curriculum enhances education by engaging the body, the imagination, and a sense of play in the learning process. Not only "kinesthetic learners" but all students can learn from the use of movement when it is combined with any and all other subjects of the curriculum (see chapter 1, "Why Movement?" for more on kinesthetic learning). The stories in this book are each linked with a related academic subject, including: science, language arts, social studies, visual art, and learning skills. Some suggestions for how to integrate these stories into the curriculum are included at the end of each story, in the section called "Extensions."

A Movement Story can be included as one of several activities of a specific learning unit, in order to generate interest in the subject and to create a springboard for further exploration of that subject. For example, in preparation for a field trip to the aquarium, the story, "Life In The Bass Lane" could be done in class. Following this, there could be a class discussion about the ocean animals in the story. The children might be asked which are their favorites and why; they then can tell what they know about these animals. The teacher could present a picture book about ocean animals. After the field trip, the students could draw pictures of the animals they saw at the aquarium. Then the class could do the Movement Story again with the variation of adding into the story new animals they've learned about and drawn. (Each story also includes suggestions for variations in order to further extend the use of the movement ideas into the curriculum.)

While movement is an invaluable tool for teaching basic curriculum, it is also an important—and often neglected—field of study in and of itself. The stories in this book are best considered as a springboard for an entire movement education program in the classroom. For more information about creating a movement education program, see "Planning A Complete Movement Lesson" at the end of this chapter, as well as chapter 2, "What Are Movement Concepts?" (including the "Idea for Exploring" each Movement Concept) and the Bibliography.

•

WHERE TO USE MOVEMENT STORIES

Movement Stories are best used in an environment that provides plenty of room to move freely and safely, with a limited amount of distractions. Clear as much space as possible, including moving furniture when necessary. You can also take your students to another space that may have more room for movement, such as a gym or music room. Movement Stories can be used outdoors as well, especially if you have padded athletic mats or a flat, grassy place.

Movement Stories can also be used in a small, limited environment. The movements can be restricted to staying in one place—Self-space—rather than moving through the General Space of the room. An example of a story that takes place entirely in Self-space is "The Mice Go To The Zoo." Another option for a small movement environment is to have half the class watch while the other half does the movements and then switch roles. Watching movement is in itself a valuable learning tool, especially if you can teach the children to focus their observations. (For example, say: "Watch how the children are moving on different levels. Can you tell when they change from high to low?")

•

HOW TO USE MOVEMENT STORIES

Practical Steps For Using These Stories:

1. Read the first two chapters, "Why Movement?" and "What Are Movement Concepts?"

2. Select a story. Your choice can be based on any of the following:
    a. The Movement Concepts you'd like to work with (see Chart of Movement Stories and the Concepts They Cover, following this chapter)

b. The story content as it relates to current classroom subjects (see "Related Academic Subject" at the beginning of each story)

    c. Whatever else sparks your interest

3. Study the Movement Concepts for the selected story in chapter 2, "What Are Movement Concepts?"

4. Read the entire story and the suggestions that follow it. Read it again slowly while doing all the movements yourself.

5. Whenever possible, memorize the story, or at least the basic outline of it. See specifics in the section below, "Memorizing Movement Stories."

6. Select the music (where applicable). The music selections listed in the appendices for each story are suggestions only—feel free to select other music or to create your own. It's also possible to do any of these stories without music.

7. Present the story to your students, keeping in mind our suggestions described below. In your presentation, include the introduction for the story. The introductions that precede each story are intended to help students understand the vocabulary words for the Movement Concepts involved.

8. After doing the story with your class, you may want to ask your students for feedback (see the end of the section, "Presenting Movement Stories," for more on student feedback). Read the Variations and Extensions suggestions listed at the end of the story and consider these and other ideas for doing the same story again in the future.

•

MEMORIZING MOVEMENT STORIES

It's possible to simply read these Movement Stories aloud, without either memorizing them or moving with the children. It's also possible to employ a method for reading the stories aloud while still being mostly free to move. However, we strongly recommend that for optimal usage these stories be memorized and that the teacher do the movements with the children (see "Moving With The Stories," below).

You don't have to memorize every word—you can paraphrase it if you know the basic story line and the movements which are included. Two stories in this collection, however, are written as poems ("Life In The Bass Lane" and "The Sculptor Who Couldn't Decide What To Make") and as such require memorization of the words as written in order to get the full effect of the rhythm and rhymes.

If memorizing the story is difficult or too time-consuming for you, you have several options. One is to simply hold the book in one hand or place it on a stand. You could also place the text of the story on index cards which you can carry with you while you do the movements. You could either handwrite the story or photocopy it and paste it onto the cards. Another option is to write only key phrases of the story on the cards. As long as you get the gist of the story, paraphrasing it is completely legitimate and will add the extra spin of your own storytelling style.

Yet another option is to write the text of the story, or key phrases from it, on poster board which you hang on the wall. You can use this technique to your advantage by using the stories as part of a language skills activity, perhaps asking the students to hunt for certain letters or words on the poster board or having them memorize one of the stories that is written in poetry form. After the children have memorized one of the stories, other elements can be added to it, such as playing percussion instruments or making sound effects along with the story.

Memorizing a story gives you the advantage of being able to fully observe the children, without being distracted by needing to read something. In this way, you can take advantage of Movement Stories as an opportunity to study your students' coordination, motor skills, kinesthetic sensibilities, social interations, and aesthetic expressiveness.

⋅

MOVING WITH THE STORIES

Memorizing the stories and moving with them will increase your ability to manage the activity of your group. For this reason, all specific movement directions—written in italics in the stories—are directed to the teacher, as well as the children. By placing yourself in the midst of their movement activity, with an understanding of where the story is going next and while not being distracted by reading it, you will be better able to shift the activity or energy if necessary.

Here's an example: You're presenting "Kids in Toyland" and the children are spinning as dreidels. You realize that they are becoming overly excited by the spinning and you want to shift the energy. You immediately calm the children by skipping ahead to the next part of the story where they sink slowly into big, soft teddy bears. You do this movement yourself while pausing the flow of the story for a few seconds, speaking in a low, soothing voice, describing the mobiles you imagine are hanging from the ceiling of the toy store. Perhaps the children describe their imaginary mobiles. When you feel the energy of the group is calmer, you continue to the next part of the story.

When you move with the stories yourself, you model the movements and shapes you are speaking about, thereby giving the children visual cues in addition to the verbal ones. Children learn in many ways and for some, "One picture is worth a thousand words," especially when the movement vocabulary is new to them. A visual model—your own movements—associated with the words helps children develop movement vocabulary.

Your movements will also give support to children who are shy about moving. They appreciate when adults do things with them, rather than talking at them, and they will enjoy your participation so much. You will too!

⋅

PRESENTING MOVEMENT STORIES

Be dramatic! Both you and your students will enjoy the stories immensely if you are expressive in your storytelling. You can help your students focus their attention by modulating your voice. Raising or lowering the volume of your voice, especially the latter, will help to shift their attention when necessary.

The stories are formatted with spaces between each movement activity. Consider the spaces as pauses. Allow the children to move during each pause, without needing to hurry to the next piece of story text. How long you pause between each movement is something you'll have to gauge for yourself and you'll learn to judge this only by active experimentation. As a general rule, if the children are moving with creativity and interest, allow them time to move. Too often, teachers assume they must be constantly talking and moving the activity forward. A pause of half a minute or more is not unreasonable, but neither is it required. The length of the pauses you take depend on the story itself, the attention span and age of your students, and how the children are interacting with the story.

During the pauses in story text, make observations aloud about the children's movements, such as, "I see Lila making a big 'O' shape with her arms overhead. I notice Joe is making a small 'O' with his fingers." Making observations aloud while the children are moving helps them to be aware of their own bodies and movements and encourages them to create new ways of moving.

It's best to make simple observations of their movements ("I see Katie is skipping lightly and quickly") rather than judgments ("Good skipping, Katie!") because it's not up to the teacher to value one child's expression over another's. Instead of judging the quality of their individual expressions of a particular movement, simply look at whether or not they are doing what you've asked them to do—are they fulfilling the movement task?

Praise or criticism teaches children to depend on an external authority for their sense of self-worth, whereas nonjudgmental observations lead them to pay attention to their actions without evaluating themselves as "good" or "bad." The act of speaking aloud your observations of their movements, while saying their names, helps build self-esteem because the children know they are being seen and appreciated by you—and that's enough. Speaking the children's names while making your observations aloud is also important for it lets them know that you see them as valued individuals and makes them feel special. Train yourself to continually make observations of individual children, speaking their names, during their movement activities.

After presenting a story, you may want to ask your students what they liked or disliked about it. Their feedback can help you understand whether or not the story met the developmental needs of your students. An enthusiastic response to a story indicates that the movements involved were both appealing and appropriate for your group. If, however, the children were frustrated with a movement task, that tells you that the movement was probably beyond their ability at this stage in their development. Feedback from your students about a particular Movement Story, including their suggestions for possible variations, will give you ideas for doing it differently in the future. Consider the Variations and Extensions ideas listed at the end of the story, for potential use in the future.

•

SETTING THE STAGE: RULES AND EXPECTATIONS

Children love Movement Stories because the stories engage their imaginations and sense of dramatic play with fun movements. Expect that your students will get excited, laugh, call out ideas, and move vigorously! When children do Movement Stories they are learning actively, rather than passively (reading or listening to the teacher), so you can expect a high level of energy. Also expect that they will want to repeat the stories again and again and again....

Before you begin, establish a special set of behavioral guidelines specifically for movement activities. The children can help create these rules. It's wise to establish a signal for "freeze," such as a certain word or a sound (for example, a drumbeat or hand clap). The "freeze" signal will help focus their attention quickly when needed. In general, when using Movement Stories, you can employ the same classroom management techniques you normally use. Your own methods of working with children and a clear sense of your own "comfort zone" for sound and activity are best for you when doing movement activities.

The concept of Self-space is a good one to start with (see "The Mice Go To The Zoo") because it teaches the children to be aware of their "kinesphere," an imaginary "bubble" around their bodies that protects themselves and others from getting hurt. The first and foremost rule is to keep hands and feet to oneself, not touching others (interactive movement can come later, with more experienced children).

Some other good, basic rules we recommend for doing Movement Stories with young children are:
1.) Listen,
2.) Be gentle, and
3.) Do your best.

●

WORKING WITH DIFFERENT AGE GROUPS

Expect that different age groups will respond differently to Movement Stories. Three-year-olds and early four- year-olds generally have short attention spans. For them, make the pauses between movements shorter and tell the stories at a slightly quicker pace than for older children. Younger children also need you to do a lot of modeling of the movements so that they can imitate you. They may not be able to do all of the movements or shapes and that's okay—just attempting them and learning the vocabulary is enough for this age group.

Four- and five-year-olds are able to dance freely for a longer period of time. For them, you can make the pauses in the story a little longer and draw out the length of the entire story a bit more. Older four- and five-year-olds will start to create their own movement ideas rather than simply imitating yours. Five- and six-year-olds will increasingly be able to come up with original ideas about movements and shapes and can invent creative alternatives for the story.

●

NONJOINERS

Some children may not want to participate, preferring to watch instead. This is perfectly all right. They can learn a lot by observing and they may be more involved in the activity than their bodies show. Gently encourage nonjoiners to participate but otherwise allow them to simply watch. Chances are that they will join in eventually when they see how much fun it is.

Nonjoining is not acceptable if it's being used as a manipulative ploy, in order to garner more negative attention. In this case, handle the situation as you would normally, whether that means ignoring them, removing them from the group, or using some other method that works for you.

●

PLANNING A COMPLETE MOVEMENT LESSON

It is our hope that educators and parents will be so inspired by Movement Stories that they will realize the necessity for movement education in child development and will want to include a comprehensive movement education program in their curricula. The following are suggestions for planning a complete half-hour to one-hour movement class for children aged three through six. Any class should include the following components:

1. Warmup:

A brief warmup serves to focus children on movement, as well as to prepare young bodies for moving. There are many suggestions for rhyming warmups in Anne Green Gilbert's *Creative Dance for All Ages,* or you can create your own.

2. Concept Introduction:

Introduce your students to the Movement Concept of the day by having them say the concept words while briefly experiencing the movements or shapes. For example, when being introduced to the concept of Size, the children would say the words "big," "medium" and "little," while making shapes of these sizes with their bodies. To see other examples, read the introductions of Movement Concepts included at the beginning of each story in this book. You can also use the information in the chapter "What Are Movement Concepts?" to guide you in introducing concepts to your students.

3. Concept Exploration:

In this section of the lesson, children have the opportunity to initially explore the concept and discover how it affects their movement. Concept explorations should be kept simple as this may be the child's first exposure to the concept being introduced. There is a suggested concept exploration activity for each Movement Concept under the heading "Idea for Exploring" in chapter 2, "What Are Movement Concepts?"

4. Skill Development:

In a well-rounded movement class, it is important to include not only opportunities for creative exploration, but also activities for the development of physical skills. The skill development section of the lesson could include one or more of the following:

    a. Rhythm skills: developing a sense of rhythm through playing musical instruments or moving to rhythmic chants.

    b. Locomotor and Nonlocomotor skills: practicing age-appropriate skills such as galloping, jumping, hopping, sliding, floating, turning, slashing, and so on. (For more ideas, see chart, "A Partial Listing of Locomotor and Nonlocomotor Movements," located at the beginning of Chapter 2, "What Are Movement Concepts?")

    c. Leaping: developing the skill of leaping by stacking objects such as milk cartons or large blocks for the children to leap over. Leaping into the air is fun and exciting and encourages development of both sides of the body through taking off from one foot and landing on the other.

d. Movement combinations: practicing a sequence of movements or a "dance." This requires children to remember instructions and to learn to link movements together. A movement combination could be a simple folk dance, a children's activity song (i.e., "Here We Go 'Round the Mulberry Bush"), or a dance you create by making a sentence of locomotor and nonlocomotor words. For such a dance you could say, for example, "Melt…roll…rise…hop… turn."

It is important to teach skills by referring to the concept introduced at the beginning of the lesson. For example, if you are teaching the concept of Level (High, Middle, and Low) you might have the children play musical instruments on low and high levels, practice slithering (low level) and leaping (high level), and/or do a simple dance that changes levels. Activities such as these will develop skills that reinforce the Movement Concept.

5. Free Dance:

A period of free dancing allows children to integrate the concept they have explored and the skills they have developed and to use them as a means of self expression. A free dance should have a fairly open structure. For example, a free dance for the concept Weight might be simply dancing lightly with scarves when the music is soft and dancing strongly with scarves when the music is loud. Children should feel free to create their own responses within the boundaries of the structure.

•

WHERE DO MOVEMENT STORIES FIT IN?

A Movement Story can fit into several sections of the complete lesson format described above. (However, it is highly recommended that you use only one Movement Story per lesson.)

A Movement Story can provide an excellent Concept Exploration, providing you choose a story that clearly articulates the concept you are introducing. For example, for working with the concept of Direction, the story "The Naughty Shoes" is a good choice because it includes all six of the directions and names them. For the concept of Weight, "Astronauts In Outer Space" provides a clear experience of both strong and light weight.

Movement Stories which are highly structured can work well for the Skill Development portion of the lesson. "The Alphabet Adventures of Little Letter O," for example, provides experience in the skill of making letter shapes, while "The Mice Go To The Zoo" can be used to develop flexibility and body awareness.

A Movement Story can also provide a fun free dance activity. For this part of the lesson, use a story that has a great deal of room for divergent movement responses, such as "The Painter and the Elves" or "The Monkey and the Dots." Stories that contain their own free dance period are most useful here.

Movement Stories
and the Concepts they Cover

	Alphabet	Astronauts	Toyland	Life/Bass	Mice	Monkey	Shoes	Painter	Pickle	Sculptor
Parts								X		
Shape	X				X					X
Balance										X
Place				X	X					
Level								X	X	
Direction		X				X				X
Pathway								X		
Size				X						
Relationship									X	
Speed			X							
Rhythm										
Weight		X								
Energy			X							
Flow										
Focus						X				

Note: Stories which explore the concepts of Rhythm and Flow have not been included in this book, as these two concepts are more abstract and complex and are best explored with more experienced movers.

THE MICE GO TO THE ZOO

by Pamela Gerke
Thanks to Anne Green Gilbert for her "foot story" idea.

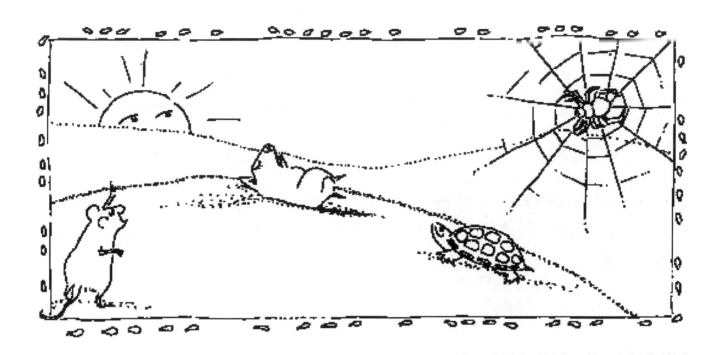

MOVEMENT CONCEPTS

Space: Self-space
Body Shape: Straight, Curved, Angular, Twisted, Wide, Narrow
Also includes stretches and Hatha Yoga postures, for flexibility of spine and limbs.

RELATED ACADEMIC SUBJECT

Science (animals)

INTRODUCTION

For our story, we'll sit in a big circle, with our legs pointed toward the center. (Make sure there is adequate space between each person.)

Imagine there's a big bubble around your body. Feel all along the inside of your bubble. The space inside your bubble is your kinesphere, the space your body takes up when you are still or moving. But be careful—if your bubble touches another bubble, it might pop! That's why we make sure there's enough room between ourselves and other people. Besides people, what else could accidently pop our bubbles? How about walls or furniture?

Each of us has our own special place in the circle, called our "self-space." In today's story we'll each stay in our own place and not move around the room. We'll be making shapes—some that are curved and some that are straight. Hold your arms straight in front of you. Now can you make them curved?

(Music—optional—begins.)

I see two little mice in front of me! *(Wiggle feet and squeak like a mouse.)*
These little mice were asleep one morning. *(Feet snore.)*
"Ahh..." *(Flex feet.)* "...Shhh..." *(Point feet.)*
"Ahh...Shhh...Ahh...Shhh..."
One little mouse woke up first and said:
"It's a beautiful day!" and danced for joy! "La, la, la, la!" *(One foot dances in the air.)*

But the other little mouse was still asleep.
"Ahh...Shhh...Ahh...Shhh..."

The first mouse tried to wake the other mouse up: *(One foot taps other foot lightly.)*
"Wake up! Wake up, sleepyhead!"
But the little mouse didn't wake up.
"Ahh...Shhh...Ahh...Shhh..."

So the first mouse tried jumping on it.
But still, the other mouse slept!
"Ahhh...Shhh...Ahh...Shhh..."

The first mouse went and got an alarm clock.
(Pantomime getting clock and pressing it against the other foot.)
RRRRRRRING!!!

And still, the other mouse slept!
"Ahh...Shhh...Ahh...Shhh..."

Finally, the first mouse ran up the leg, slid all the way down, and bounced on the sleeping mouse! The other mouse finally woke up and said:

"Hey, what's going on?"
"Time to get up! It's a beautiful day!"
"Okay, but first we have to do our exercises!"

"Stretch forward." *(Point feet.)*
"Stretch backward." *(Flex feet.)*
(Repeat.)
"Stretch in big circles around and around." *(Circle feet, keeping heels on the floor.)*
"Now around and around the other way."

"10 push-ups! 1-2-3-4-5-6-7-8-9-10!" *(Keeping balls of feet on the floor, lift heels.)*

"10 jumping jacks! 1-2-3-4-5-6-7-8-9-10!" *(Clap feet together.)*

"Okay, now what should we do?"
"Let's go to the zoo!"
"Yippee!!"

The rest of their family was still asleep, so they tiptoed out of the house. *(Tiptoe in place.)*
Once they got outside, they were so happy that they skipped! *(Skip in place.)*
"La, la, la, la!"

When they arrived at the zoo, the mice climbed to the top of a tall tree in order to see everything better.
(Slowly lift legs, knees straight and hands pressing the floor at your sides. Slowly lower legs to the floor.)

The first thing they saw were some giraffes. The giraffes' necks were so long that they reached to the sky! *(Stretch arms up.)*

When the giraffes saw some good leaves to eat in the trees, they bent over and reached for them.
(Slowly lower arms toward feet or knees, while bending at the waist.)

The little mice in the treetops squeaked with fright and leaned as far away from the mouths of those giraffes as they could!
(Point feet forward while stretching hands toward feet or knees.)

Then the giraffes raised their necks up to the sky again.
(Raise arms up again, then slowly lower to sides.)

Giraffes are herbivores, which means they only eat plants, but just the same, the mice were grateful to escape! They scurried down the tree and went to where the lions lived.
(Turn onto hands and knees, facing the center of the circle.)

The lions slowly shook their heads from side to side and roared gently.
When the lions saw the little mice they were so afraid that they arched their backs.
(Arch middle of back toward ceiling while pulling head and tail together, toward center of body.)

The mice said: "Don't be afraid! We won't hurt you!"

The lions relaxed when they heard that.
(Relax lower back while slowly pushing your bottom up and out, away from the center of your body, and raising up your head. Roar gently.)

Just then, the lions saw something that frightened them, and again they arched their backs.
(Repeat as before.)

The mice told them: "Don't be such scaredy-cats! It's only a ladybug!"
The lions relaxed again. *(Repeat as before.)*

Next, the mice went to the Reptile House to see the snakes.
(Slither on stomach in place for a few moments.)

There they saw a cobra!
(Lie on stomach, head toward the center of circle, legs straight, and forehead resting on the floor. Place palms flat underneath shoulders, elbows bent and close to your sides.)

The cobra lifted up it's head and looked right at them!
(Slowly raise upper torso by pushing hands on the floor and slowly straightening elbows, keeping pelvis on the floor. Flick tongue like a snake.)

Then the cobra turned and looked behind itself.
(Lower torso slightly by bending your elbows and slowly turning head to look behind you.)

The cobra turned and looked the other way behind itself.

Then it faced forward again and slowly lowered to the floor.
(Turn head to face forward while straightening elbows and raising upper torso. Slowly lower torso to the floor by bending elbows.)

In the Reptile House there were some turtles with big, round backs.
(Crouch on hands and knees, arching back into a rounded shape.)

The mice were very naughty and they pushed the turtles over onto their backs!
(Gently roll over onto back, bend knees and hug them to your chest.)

The turtles tried to roll over! They rocked from side to side.
They rocked forward and backward.

The turtles cried out: "Help! Help! We can't turn over!"

The mice felt sorry for them and pushed them upright again.
(Roll over onto hands and knees again.)

The mice now went to see the spiders. *(Sit upright.)*
They saw a spider that was all curled up in a little ball.
(Draw arms and legs in toward center of the body.)

Then the spider yawned and stretched out all its legs.
(Stretch out limbs: legs form a "V" shape on the floor, arms raised overhead.)

With a sigh, the spider curled up in a ball again…*(Repeat as before.)*
And then yawned and stretched out its legs again. *(Repeat as before.)*
The mice decided it was time to go home.
"Let's race!"
And they ran all the way home! *(Run feet in place.)*

When they got home they took a little nap and rested for their next adventure.
"Ah...Shhh...Ah...Shhh..."

(Music ends. End of Story.)

MUSICAL SUGGESTIONS

Calm, quiet, background music

Deuter, "Call of the Unknown," *Call of the Unknown*

Hap Palmer, *Seagulls* (any selection)

SUGGESTIONS FOR PRESENTATION

For this story, the teacher should model all the shapes and movements by doing them with the children. It's best to memorize the story or write the sequence on cards which you can lay on the floor in front of you, so that you are free to move without the interruption of reading the book. The children should be spread far enough apart from each other to give them plenty of room to move without bumping into their neighbors.

If you're not used to doing stretches and Hatha Yoga postures, here are some basic guidelines: GO SLOWLY. Stretch your body only as far as you can without feeling pain. If you do stretches every day, they become easier and over time you will find that you're able to stretch farther and for a longer period of time. Remember to keep taking slow, full breaths while stretching and holding postures. Wear loose, comfortable clothes.

Have fun with the mouse voices! The children will enjoy making their own squeaky mouse sounds.

VARIATIONS

Ask the children to make suggestions for the mice's exercises and adventures. What else can the first mouse do to try to wake up the other mouse? The feet can play other characters as well, such as rabbits or elves.

If you are familiar with other stretches or postures, you can include them in this story, or in a story of your own invention. For example, when you lift up your legs as the giraffes are reaching into the treetops, you can lift your legs even higher by lying on your back and raising up your hips until you can support them with your hands, elbows pressed against the floor. (In Hatha Yoga, this pose is called, *Viparita Karani,* or "Simple Inverted Pose," also known as "The Candle.")

Another variation is to do this story, or variations of it, at regular intervals, such as once or twice a week, and slowly increase the length of time each pose is held, thereby increasing the beneficial effects to blood circulation, heart rate, and general calming of the mind and spirit. You can make a game of it by counting the seconds each pose is held.

COMMENTARY

This story is a good one to do when you want to calm and center the energy of your group. The story is all done in self-space and in sitting positions and does not include any vigorous activity or movement in general space. It can be done when your physical space is small and you don't have a lot of room for movement. The stretches and postures included in this story are basic for any physical warm-up and can be practiced daily or before other physical activities, such as dance or P.E.

Some Yogis say: "The key to happiness is a flexible spine." With all of the time our modern-day children spend watching TV and sitting at computers, movement activities that keep the body flexible and limber are essential for good development and, yes, happiness.

The "cobra" position, *Bhujangasana,* is an especially good backward bend for the upper spine. (It also reduces flatulence!) Each posture should be followed by it's opposite in order to maximize flexibility; therefore, in this story the "cobra" backward bend is followed by arching the back (the turtles). Another example in this story of bending the spine in opposite directions is the lions, who arch their backs toward the ceiling and then relax them in the opposite direction. The lions' back stretch is excellent for maintaining suppleness to the lower back. Practicing this stretch daily will reduce lower back problems.

EXTENSION

This story can be a springboard for establishing a regular physical warm-up and stretching practice for your group. Due to the calming nature of this type of practice, "foot stories" and stories that incorporate stretches and postures can become a regular activity that focuses the attention of the group, such as whenever the group gathers at the beginning of the day, or after recess.

This story can also be included as part of a study of animals or a field trip to the zoo. What other animal shapes can the children make? Are the shapes straight or curved?

•

THE SCULPTOR WHO COULDN'T DECIDE WHAT TO MAKE

by Pamela Gerke

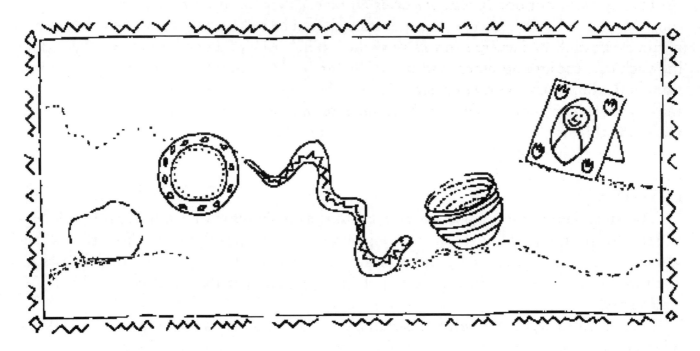

MOVEMENT CONCEPTS
Body Shape: Straight, Curved, Angular, Twisted, Wide, Narrow
Direction: Forward, Backward, Sideways, Up, Down
Balance: On Balance, Off Balance

RELATED ACADEMIC CONCEPT
Visual Art (shape)

INTRODUCTION
In this story, you will be making all kinds of shapes with your body. I would like to see you make some of these shapes before we begin:

Make a wide shape with your legs. Stretch your arms into a narrow shape over your head. In this shape your arms are very straight. Now can you make them curved? Next, bend your knees and elbows—this makes an "angular" shape.

Right now, your shapes look "on balance." That means you aren't going to fall over.

Can you stay on balance if you stand on only one leg?

Now, let's go off balance. Tip, then fall!

In our story you will also be moving in different directions. Let's try some directions:

Walk forward…jump backward…slide sideways…hop up…sit down.

•

(Begin with children sitting on the floor in self-space.)

Hello, I'm a sculptor.
I'm happy to meet you!
But can you please tell me:
What does a sculptor do? *(Children answer.)*

I sculpt with clay. But where is my clay?
I thought I left it around here today…
Ah, here's a lump of clay! *(Pat child.)*
And another! And another! *(And so forth. Pat each child.)*

Now I have plenty of clay!
But it's too dry and hard for play.
Doggone it,
I'll have to sprinkle water on it! *(Pantomime sprinkling the children.)*

Now, to soften the clay
I'll knead it every which way: *(Sit on the floor and lean in the directions called.)*
I push it forward…Backward…Forward…Backward.
I push it to one side…Then to the other side.

Side to side. Side to side.
Now I'll press it down flat
And the clay spreads out wide. *(Lie on the floor, making a wide shape.)*

Now I've made a plate!
But what else can I make?
I know! I'll roll it into
A long, skinny snake!

Roll, roll, roll the snake
To make it long and narrow, *(Roll on the floor in a long "snake" shape.)*
I pull the top… *(Stretch arms over head on the floor.)*
And stretch the bottom… *(Point feet.)*
To make it straight as an arrow!

Straight is nice… but what else can I do
With this long and narrow roll?
I think I'll curve it 'round and 'round,
And coil it into a bowl! *(Curve body into a "C" or "O" shape.)*

But do I really want a bowl?
I can't make up my mind!
If I twist my clay like so,
I can make a pretzel design! *(Twist body or limbs any which way.)*

My power with clay is awesome,
I can do anything you name!
I can bend it with sharp angles
To make a picture frame! *(Bend arms or legs to make some kind of frame.)*
I can unbend it instead
And make it stand on it's head!
(Try standing on your head, or just pretend. Children may try different ways, such as cartwheels or on hands and knees, head touching the floor.)

Or roll it in a ball… *(Curl body into a ball.)*
…Or make a statue tall! *(Stand up.)*
But this statue is off balance…
Uh, oh! It's starting to fall! *(Fall over.)*

Again, I make it stand… *(Stand up.)*
But it falls to one side! *(Fall to one side.)*
Now I make it balanced
By spreading it's feet wide. *(Stand up and spread legs apart.)*

Now, statues are something I really love.
But can you tell me:
What are you a statue of?
(Children can say what kind of statue they are.)

Now it's time to put my clay away.
I'll mush it up, *(Wiggle body.)*
Form it into a lump, *(Sit on the floor.)*
And save it for another day!
Thanks, clay!
(End of story.)

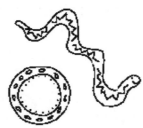

MUSICAL SUGGESTIONS

Soft, light background music (optional):
Richard Warner, *Quiet Heart*
Shadowfax, "Dreams of Children," *Dreams of Children*

SUGGESTIONS FOR PRESENTATION

Speak the poem with a sense of rhythm and musicality. Pause between each verse, allowing the children plenty of time to form each shape while you make observations about their shapes. There are many ways to make the shapes in this story and the children will invent a variety of bowl, pretzel and frame shapes. By observing aloud what individual children are doing, you will give all of them new ideas to try. For example, "I see Madison making a pretzel shape with his arms, Alec is twisting his legs like a pretzel, and Steven has twisted his whole body into a pretzel." While pausing between verses you can also give the children suggestions for making shapes, such as, "How big a bowl could you make if you joined your snake shape with someone else's?" or, "Can you make a teeny tiny statue?"

VARIATIONS

Encourage the children to comment on their shapes by asking them questions such as: "What are you going to put in your bowl?," "What picture will you put in the frame?" or, "Tell me about your statue."

Allow individuals to take turns as the sculptor. The "sculptor" can decide what shapes she or he wants the "clay" to form and either describe the shapes with words, and/or physically mold you or other students into the shapes. It's empowering and enjoyable for children to be in control of a creative activity, especially when the teacher participates. Students will love having you be one of the lumps of clay!

The concept of Balance can be explored further by having each shape (plate, snake, bowl, and so on) go off balance and tip over. Ask the children what it is about their shape that makes it tip over in the first place—is it lopsided? What do they need to change about their shape in order to be on balance?

COMMENTARY

The use of rhythm and rhyme sparks interest and the natural musicality in children. Rhythm and rhyme are wonderful tools for teaching vocabulary and other language skills.

EXTENSIONS

Directions can be emphasized and reinforced in many ways. When your group goes somewhere, such as outside for recess, the teacher can give directional commands ("Walk backward. Gallop forward. Jump sideways.") Remember that, as a Movement Concept, "direction" is different from "facing." Direction is determined by the surface of the body which is leading us through space while facing is determined by the place in the room that the front of your body is facing. (see chapter, "What Are Movement Concepts" on Direction). Children can also practice traveling through the classroom in various directions.

Body shapes can be incorporated into other classroom activities. When learning numerals, challenge the children to make the numeral shapes with their bodies. Have them describe their shapes as either Straight, Curved, Angular, Twisted, Wide, or Narrow. You can do the same thing for learning alphabet letters.

Use rhythm and rhyme in the classroom often. Read poems to your students while allowing them to move freely to the rhythms. Make up simple phrases that end with rhymes. Leave the last word off the end of a phrase and ask the children to choose their own rhyming word to end it. For example: "Today we will make/A small, fruit shape/It's round and purple/It's called a _____ (grape)." Teach the children some of the rhyming lines of the "Sculptor" story so that they can speak it in unison while forming these shapes. Pass out percussion instruments and ask some or all of the children to accompany this poem with percussion.

An art project with clay is a natural extention of this story. The children can make shapes with their clay or modeling clay and then form the same shapes with their bodies, or vice versa.

•

THE ALPHABET ADVENTURES
OF LITTLE LETTER O

by Helen Landalf
inspired by an idea by Anne Green Gilbert

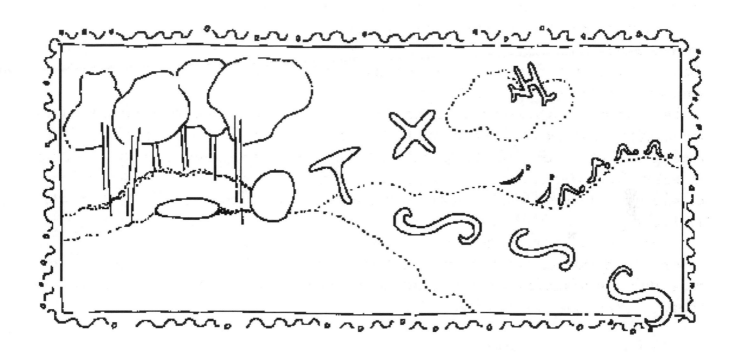

MOVEMENT CONCEPT

Shapes: Straight, Curved, Angular, Twisted, Wide, Narrow

RELATED ACADEMIC SUBJECT

Language Arts (letters)

INTRODUCTION

Today we'll do a story that's all made out of shapes. The shapes will be letters of the alphabet. Let's make a letter O that's very round and curved.

Now try a letter T, all made out of straight lines. It's wide on the top, narrow on the bottom. We'll see what other letters we'll find in this story!

•

(Have children begin on the floor, curled into balls. Music begins.)

There was once a little round letter O who lived in a hole in the forest. One morning the O decided to go exploring, so it rolled over and over, saying "O...O...O..."

(Roll on floor, keeping body in a tight ball. Encourage children to make letter sounds along with you. Be sure to say the sound that the letter makes rather than the letter's name. With very young children, you may omit saying the letter sounds or have them say the movement word instead; in this case, "roll...roll...roll...")

The O rolled and rolled until it bumped into a tall tree. Boom!

As soon as the O touched the tree, it started to stretch. It got taller and taller, 'till it was a tall letter T. The T tiptoed and turned through the forest saying "T...T...T..." *(or "tiptoe... tiptoe...tiptoe...")*

(Children make a letter T by standing with their arms outstretched, holding this shape as they tiptoe and turn.)

The T tiptoed along until it met a balloon man. "Letter T," said the balloon man, "you're too tall and thin. Let me blow you up!" So the balloon man put some air in one of the T's arms— "Kssss..." *(The sound of the letter X.)*

(Children raise one arm higher.)

He put some air into the T's other arm—"Kssss..."

(Children raise the other arm higher, creating a letter Y.)

The Y began to yawn.

(Children stretch arms overhead, as if yawning.)

"I'm not done with you yet!" said the balloon man. He put some air into one of the T's legs— "Kssss..."

(Children step into a wider stance with one leg.)

He put some air into the T's other leg—"Kssss..."

(Children step into a wider stance with the other leg.)

Now it was an excellent letter X! The letter X began to float in the air like a wide balloon, saying "Kssss...Kssss...Kssss..."

(Children hold their letter X shape as they float slowly through the room, perhaps turning. With younger children, you may omit the sound "Kssss...")

But the letter X sprang a leak, and all the air came out: "Sssss..." Now it was a curvy letter S on the ground.

(Children sink to the floor.)

The letter S began to squiggle and squirm.
Suddenly it stretched into a long letter I.

(Children lie on their stomachs, arms stretched on the floor in front of them.)

The I began to inch through the mud, saying "Inch...inch...inch..."

(Children move like an inchworm on their stomachs, bringing their knees close to their hands, backs arched, then stretching out long.)

The I didn't want its face to get muddy, so it pushed its hands down and lifted its face out of the mud, saying "Ick!"

(Children remain on their stomachs, pressing the ground with both hands, face and chest lifted off the floor as in the yoga pose "The Cobra.")

When the I got tired of slithering, it stood up and shook all the mud off its body.

It was so happy to be out of the mud that it turned into a letter H. (Stand with legs wide and turned out to sides with bent knees. Arms are up and turned out to sides with bent elbows, hands pointing upwards.) The letter H hopped on one foot saying, "Ha...Ha....Ha..." *(or "hop...hop...hop...")*. Then it hopped on the other foot, "Ha...Ha...Ha..."

Then the H noticed that it was all by itself in the forest and it sat right down in a long letter L and said, "I'm lonely."

(Children sit with legs stretched forward, arms overhead.)

The L curled back into a little letter O and rolled over and over, back to its hole, saying, "O...O...O..." *(or "roll...roll...roll...")*

Good night, little O.

(Children are once again curled into little balls on the floor. It's nice to stroke each child's back gently as you say good night. Music ends. End of story.)

MUSICAL SUGGESTIONS

Soft, calming:

Deuter, "Call of the Unknown," *Call of the Unknown*

Shadowfax, "Dreams of Children," *Dreams of Children*

SUGGESTIONS FOR PRESENTATION

It works best for the teacher to model the letter shapes for the class, particularly if they aren't familiar with letters or are just learning them. Even children who don't know their letters, however, enjoy this story and can benefit from it.

You can encourage your students to say the letter sounds with you by modeling the sound once then saying, "Try it with me." Even children who choose not to make the sounds themselves will benefit from hearing them. As an alternative to making letter sounds, you may choose to have them verbalize the movement they are performing; i.e., "roll...roll...roll..." or "hop...hop...hop..." (See text of story for specific suggestions.) Saying the movement words may work better for young three-year-olds than making letter sounds. It is also possible to omit making sounds or saying words altogether and simply have them perform the shapes and movements suggested in the story.

VARIATIONS

Try holding up alphabet flashcards to show your students the shapes you wish them to make. Most children greatly enjoy the challenge of making letters with their bodies. Don't worry too much about them doing it "right"—accept the many variations you see and simply look for an understanding of the general essence of the letter (does it have straight lines, curved lines, and so on).

As a further challenge for children who already recognize letters, try telling the story and making the shape of each letter with your own body, allowing the students to tell you the letter's name.

COMMENTARY

This story is obviously an excellent one for developing letter recognition skills, as well as letter-sound correspondence. By making the shape of each letter with their own bodies, students gain a kinesthetic awareness of that letter's shape, rather than just a visual awareness.

The turning motions children are required to do in this story help stimulate the vestibular system which is important for developing coordination and maintaining a sense of balance. Other movements that provide this stimulation are: swinging, swaying, rocking, and spinning.

Another important developmental movement that this story encourages is the action of pushing the head and chest away from the floor, as in the Yoga position "The Cobra." This pushing motion is one of an infant's earliest movements. As discussed in Chapter 1, returning to movements from earlier developmental stages can create or strengthen neurological pathways in the brain and can be highly beneficial in enhancing a child's perceptual, motor, and cognitive skills.

EXTENSIONS

You might experiment with adding other letters to the story. How about a dancing D, a prancing P, a flitting F, a bouncing B, or a vibrating V!

Try extending the activity of making letter shapes to other parts of your classroom day. For example, students can use their bodies to "spell" the name of the month as they look at the daily calendar. Making letter shapes can become a favorite after-lunch activity.

If your class is working on alphabet skills, you may want to take photos of different students as they make letter shapes with their bodies and display them in the classroom alongside your traditional alphabet chart.

For many excellent ideas on teaching letters through movement, see *Teaching the Three Rs Through Movement Experiences* by Anne Green Gilbert (complete listing in Bibliography).

•

LIFE IN THE BASS LANE: AN UNDERSEA ADVENTURE

by Pamela Gerke

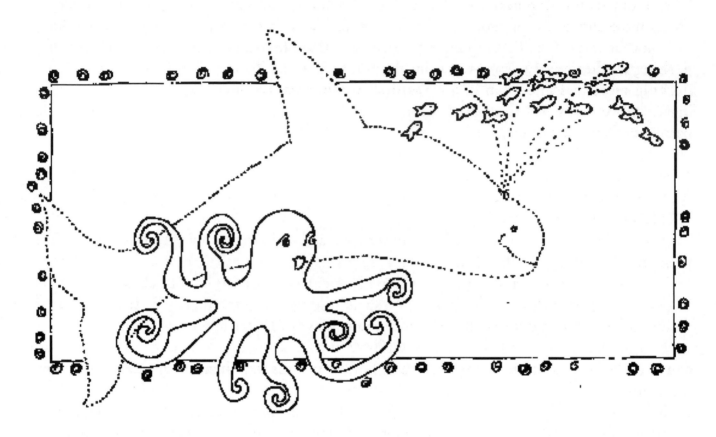

MOVEMENT CONCEPTS

Place: Self-space, General Space
Size: Big, Medium, Little

RELATED ACADEMIC SUBJECT

Science (oceanography)

INTRODUCTION

Today we're going on an undersea adventure. Some of our story will take place in Self- space—that's when we stay in one place. But we'll also be moving around the room, which is called moving in General Space.

We'll be making shapes of different sizes. When we make a big shape, our arms and legs extend far away from the center of our bodies. Make a really big shape. Now make little shape. Notice that when you make a little shape, you pull your arms and legs in close to the center of your body. What does a medium-sized shape look like?

●

(Begin with children standing.)

Walk around the room…then stop!
In your own special place
Where you can stretch
Without touching anyone:
Your own self-space.

Feel all around you
An invisible bubble. *(Use hands to "feel" the space all around you.)*
While inside it you can move,
Protected from all trouble.

Now, in your bubble, come with me
And we'll explore the mystery
Of the big, deep, blue sea…

We sink into the water, *(Slowly sink to the floor.)*
Going down, down, down,
To the bottom of the ocean
Where there's hardly any sound. *(Sit or lay down.)*

(Whisper:) Listen to the silence of the ocean….*(Pause for a few moments of silence.)*

In this watery world
We can all be
All the living creatures
That we see:

We can be an octopus *(Begin to move as octopus, waving arms and legs.)*
Sitting in self-space,
Counting all its arms
From number one to number eight: *(Move arms and legs while counting.)*
"1, 2, 3, 4, 5, 6, 7, 8."

And there, sitting by itself, too,
Is a sea anemone that's purple and blue. *(Curl up limbs toward the center of your body.)*

When it's curled up in a little ball
The anemone is very small.
But when it's hungry it begins to grow
And opens up—slow, slow…*(Slowly extend arms and legs outward.)*

And as it gets bigger in size
It starts to rise and rise…*(Slowly stand up.)*

…Until it sees something to eat,
And goes, "CHOMP!" *(Pantomime taking a huge bite, grabbing something with arms.)*
Then quickly closes up again,
Small and neat. *(Resume small, curled-up shape on the floor.)*

There's a little, baby sea bass *(Stand and crouch to make a small shape.)*
With a little, fishy face, *(Make a "fish face.")*
Swimming 'round a little rock,
In its own, little place. *(Crouching in a small shape, "swim" on two feet in a small circle.)*

It swims all by itself,
Until it learns the rule:
All little fishies
Must go to school!

Now we swim in general space,
All across the sea.
We each leave our own self-space,
To swim far and free.
("Swim" all around in general space. Encourage children to "swim" on two feet.)

Now a sea bass is very small
Compared to the largest sea creature of all.
Who is it? *(Children say what they think.)*

Yes, whales are the biggest creatures
In the mighty big sea.
Can you show me how very big
A whale can be? *(Make a big shape.)*

Whales are very sociable
And don't live all alone.
They live in groups called "pods"
In their lovely ocean home.

Can you swim in a big shape
With other big whales,
Without bumping into anyone
With your fins or your tail? *("Swim" in general space, keeping big shape.)*

(Music begins.)

Whales called "orcas"
Have a very special flair,
For these black and white mammals
Like to leap in the air!

Big, giant leaps!
Leaps that are small!
Medium-sized leaps!
And the biggest leaps of all!
Heaps and heaps of leaps!
Orca whales have lots of fun
When they leap and dance
In the air and the sun!

(Allow for a free dance period.
Music ends.)

Now dive to the floor
Of this watery place
And find some slippery eels
Slithering silently in self space… *(Sink to the floor and slither on your stomach, silently.)*

There's some cranky crabs here,
Scuttling sideways with a sigh. *("Crab walk" on hands and feet, sideways.)*
They gently bump each other—
"Excuse you!" the cranky crabs cry!

Now is the time:
To the ocean's surface we must climb.
We slowly rise to the top of the sea, *(Stand up.)*
And sway gently in the water's motion, *(Sway in place.)*
We remember all we've seen and we say:
Thank you, wonderful ocean!
We'll come again another day!
(End of story.)

MUSICAL SUGGESTIONS

Carefree, light and happy:

Esther "Little Dove" John, "Ocean Bossa," *The Elements, Volume II*

Rumbel and Tingstad, "Gigue," *Emerald*

SUGGESTIONS FOR PRESENTATION

Practice the poem so that you can speak each verse with a steady meter—the children will respond to the rhythm of it. Feel free to stop between each verse and allow time for the children to move. At these times you can make observations about the children's movements, such as, "I notice Sarah making a very small anemone shape." Or, "I see Jessie doing huge high leaps."

There are two places in the story for silence: when you first go to the bottom of the ocean and near the end when you become eels. Don't cut the silences short—teachers often feel obliged to keep up a steady stream of talk and activity, but we should also allow time for children to listen to silence.

When children pretend to swim like fish, they commonly slide on their stomachs on the floor. Encourage them to also try "swimming" in an upright position, on their feet.

VARIATIONS

For each of the different sea creatures portrayed here, you can allow time for free dance. Select different music for each sea creature and pause between each section of the poem to play music for free dance. Perhaps you'll use slow, dreamy music for an octopus dance and lively, silly music for a crab dance.

Ask the children what other animals live in the sea and what size they are. Do these animals always stay in one place—Self-space—or do they move across the General Space of the sea? Make up your own verses for other ocean creatures—maybe the children can help you with some of the rhymes.

COMMENTARY

This story uses poetry to establish a rhythmic sense of life under the sea. The music of poetry is well suited to movement activity, as well as being a valuable tool for teaching vocabulary and other language skills. Children are naturally attracted to rhythm and rhyme and they respond readily to it. Poetry creates beauty and music which is reason enough to use it in the classroom often.

This story asks the children to imagine a bubble around themselves in order to visualize the space that their own body takes up. This space is also called the kinesphere. It's important for young children to develop a sense of their kinesphere in order to maintain control over their bodies as they move in space. Having control over one's own body and movement gives children a sense of both safety and excitement. They can do so many exciting movements with their own body! Anne Green Gilbert recommends that when two children bump into each other, both freeze for five counts. During the five counts they can be looking for an empty space in the room to move to.

EXTENSIONS

This story might be a springboard for a unit on the ocean. Your class could create a bulletin board or mural about the sea and add to it their drawings of the creatures who live there.

Poetry and rhymes could also be explored further. Ask the children to think of words that rhyme. For example, you say a simple word, such as "shark" and the children try to rhyme it, with words like, "dark" and "bark." When you have a string of rhyming words, the class can make up a poem, such as: "The shark/swam in the dark/and heard the seals bark."

•

THE NAUGHTY SHOES

by Helen Landalf
inspired by an idea by Michael Clawsen

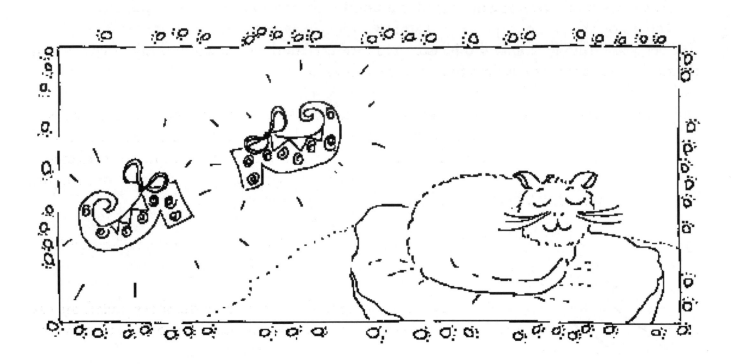

MOVEMENT CONCEPT

Directions: Forward, Backward, Right Side, Left Side, Up, Down

RELATED ACADEMIC SUBJECT

Learning Skills (directions)

INTRODUCTION

This story will make you move in many different directions. Try stretching your arms in each one of these directions:

Forward
Backward
Right
Left
Up
Down

(Begin with children laying on the floor.)

Once there was a cat. Now this was a very unusual cat because it could walk on two legs just like a person. Well, one morning this cat was all curled up in its bed, fast asleep.

The cat woke up, gave a big cat yawn, and stretched its paws in all directions: forward, backwards, sideways, up, and down.

The cat decided to go for a walk in the forest, so it jumped out of bed and started off down the road. The cat was so excited that it started to gallop.

Suddenly the cat stopped. There, in the middle of the road, were the most beautiful shoes it had ever seen! They were gold with silver sparkles, purple polka dots, and green shoelaces. "I think I'll try them on," said the cat. So it put the beautiful shoes on its feet. They fit perfectly. But when the cat tried to walk, the shoes did something surprising: They walked backwards. Faster, faster, faster…until the cat fell down.

"You naughty shoes!" said the cat. "I'd better try again." But this time the shoes started sliding sideways. Right… left… right… left… right… left…until the cat fell down.

"You naughty shoes!" said the cat. "I'd better try again." But this time the shoes pulled the cat up and down. Up to the sky *(Tiptoe.)*, down to the ground *(Crouch.)* Up to the sky, down to the ground. Up to the sky, down to the ground…until the cat fell down.

"You naughty shoes!" said the cat. "I'll give you ONE MORE CHANCE." Would you like to say that with me? *(Children repeat with you.)*

But this time the shoes began to spin and turn and twirl the cat 'round and 'round…until the cat fell down.

By now, the cat was angry. "These shoes are just too naughty!" it said. So the cat took the shoes off and set them down in the middle of the road. Then the cat started to walk away.

But, stop! *(Freeze.)* I hear something.

The cat listened, but nobody was there. So it kept on walking.

Stop! I hear something.

The cat listened, but there was nobody there. So it kept walking.

Stop! I hear something!

The cat turned around quickly and saw that the shoes were following it down the road. So the cat started to chase the shoes:
Forward!
Sideways!
'Round and 'Round!

Finally the cat grabbed the shoes. "Now I've got you, you naughty shoes. This time, walk forward." The cat put the shoes back on its feet and sure enough, the shoes walked forward just like they were supposed to.

(Music begins.)

The cat was so happy that it did a happy little dance in all directions: forward, backward, sideways, up and down, 'round and 'round.

(Allow a brief period for free dancing. Fade music slowly when children appear to be finished with their dance. Music ends.)
The happy cat galloped all the way home in its new shoes.

The cat climbed into bed and took off the shoes.
It gave each shoe a little kiss, then put them under the pillow.
Then the cat fell fast asleep. Good night, cat. Good night, shoes.
(End of story.)

MUSICAL SELECTIONS

Fun, fast-moving:

Hap Palmer, "Funky Penguin," *Movin'*

James Galway, "Le Basque," *Annie's Song*

SUGGESTIONS FOR PRESENTATION

Children really enjoy the naughtiness of the shoes, especially if you let each set of movements get faster and faster. You can cue this with the speed of your speaking voice. For example, when saying, "Right, left, right, left, right, left," let the change of direction happen a little more quickly each time. It's also fun to let the sense of urgency accelerate during the "Stop. I hear something" section. The more unexpected and tricky you make the events seem, the more engaged your students will be.

It's great to give children the opportunity to move freely for a short period when the cat is doing its happy dance. The key to making this successful is fun, energetic music (see suggestions above), and your calling out suggestions and giving positive comments as they are moving. As the children dance, feed them with new ideas: "Can you move backwards down low? How about big and little steps sideways?" You are not demanding that they produce these movements; you are opening their minds to possibilities which they may or may not choose to try at the moment. Also try verbalizing what you observe or what you'd like to see: "Look at those arms moving in all different directions!"

How do you know when to end a period of free dancing? Watch your students. They will tell you, through their movements, when they are becoming tired, distracted, or are running out of ideas. For a young, inexperienced group this may happen after only thirty seconds. Other groups are able to dance freely for two to three minutes at a time. Try fading the music gradually just as the dance seems to be dissolving. You don't want to cut their exploration short but you also want to avoid utter chaos. The more a group practices dancing freely the longer their dance periods will become and the more creative their movement will be.

COMMENTARY

The skill of moving backward is a difficult one because you cannot see where you are going. If a child is having trouble moving backward, it sometimes helps to pull gently on the back of his or her shirt to help guide them.

With young children it's best not to be too concerned about the idea of right and left. You may say the words so that they'll become familiar with them but you don't need to correct children who are moving the "wrong" way. They will understand the concept when they are ready. It's also fine to just say "side to side" instead of "right and left."

VARIATIONS

Instead of focusing on the concept of Directions, you could make this a story about Pathways, with the shoes making the cat move in straight, curved, or zigzag pathways. It can also be a story about Speed (fast and slow), Size (big and little), or Quality (smooth and sharp). Just vary the movements the shoes make the cat do. Perhaps your students can give you suggestions for different kinds of shoes and how they might make the cat move. For help with this, see the Movement Concepts chart at the beginning of the chapter "What Are Movement Concepts?" You could also vary this story by having the cat find a pair of gloves, a hat, a pair of pants, or…?

EXTENSIONS

Your students might like to help you create a story about the further adventures of the cat and its shoes. Where did the cat go the next day? What did it find there? Were the shoes naughty again, or did they help the cat escape some danger? You may want to sit down with your class and create a story together, then get up and translate it into movement.

•

THE PAINTER AND THE ELVES

by Helen Landalf

MOVEMENT CONCEPTS

Body Parts: Hands, Feet, Head, Elbows, Backs, and so on
Levels: High, Middle, Low
Pathways: Straight, Curved, Zigzag

RELATED ACADEMIC SUBJECT

Visual Art (line)

INTRODUCTION

In our story today we'll be moving in different pathways. Pathways are like designs we paint on the floor or in the air with our body parts. Right where we are, let's try painting a straight pathway in the air with our hands…

A curved pathway with our head…

A zigzag pathway with our elbow.

(It's very helpful to have visual examples of each kind of pathway to show the students. You can draw a straight line, a curved line, and a zigzag line on the chalkboard or on a piece of paper which you pin on the bulletin board.)

•

(Before beginning the story, instruct children to "hide" together in a corner of the room.)

Once upon a time, there was a painter who loved to paint. She (or he) had many cans of paint of different colors spread out on the floor of her room. She had red paint, blue paint, yellow paint, green paint—all the colors of the rainbow.

Every night before the painter went to bed she put lids on her cans of paint so they wouldn't dry out. But one night she was so sleepy that she forgot to put the lids on. And who should sneak into the room that very night but some little elves.

(Motion for children to come out of their hiding place. Music begins.)

Well, when the elves saw the cans of paint, they were very excited. Each elf went over to a can of paint (each child finds a place to stand) and stuck one hand in it. They pulled out their hands to look. They were beautiful!
Next the elves stuck their heads in the paint. They got paint all over their hair.
Then they stuck their elbows in the paint.
They sat down in the paint and wiggled their bottoms.
Last of all, each elf jumped right into a can of paint and got paint all over its body.

Then the elves had a wonderful idea. "Let's paint the room and surprise the painter when she wakes up!" So they jumped right out of the cans and began skating straight pathways all over the room, like stripes.

They ran in curved pathways, painting letter "S"s or snakes on the floor.
They jumped in zigzags, making lightning designs with their feet.

Then the elves got right down on a low level and began to slither paint all over the floor with their tummies…and their backs…and even their sides.
They scooted designs with their bottoms.
They painted polka dots with their elbows and knees.

"Hey, we almost forgot to paint the ceiling!"said the elves, so they lept high in the air, flicking paint onto the ceiling with their fingers.

Soon the morning sun began to come up and all the elves hurried back to their hiding places.

(Music ends.)

When the painter woke up and saw her room, she couldn't believe her eyes. There were straight, curved, and zigzag designs all over the floor. There were even polka dots on the ceiling!

"Those naughty elves," she said. "They used my paint without asking my permission. I'm going to teach them a lesson."

So she emptied out all the cans of paint, and filled them with sticky glue.

Well, the next night when the painter was asleep, who should sneak into the room again, but those naughty little elves.

(Motion for children to enter. Music begins.)

They went right up to the cans of paint and without even looking they stuck one hand in. Their hands were stuck in the glue! They swung the paint cans from side to side but they wouldn't come off.

So they each stuck a foot in the can to help pull it off. But now their feet were stuck, too! The poor elves had to hop around the room on one foot.
Just then, in walked the painter.

(Music ends.)

"You naughty elves," she said. "You used my paint without asking me first. But I can see that you're sorry, so I'll pull you out of the glue."

So, one by one, she pulled each elf out of its can. Then all the elves ran home.

(Gently lift each child a few inches off the ground for a moment. Then the children run back to their hiding places.)

And do you know—those elves never used the painter's paint without asking, ever again.
(End of story.)

MUSICAL SUGGESTIONS
Sprightly, magical:
    Debussy, *Suite from Peleas and Melisande*
    Brewer, Rumble, and Tingstad, "Fisherman's Dream," *Emerald*

SUGGESTIONS FOR PRESENTATION
Children enjoy this story immensely if the teacher plays the role of the painter, yawning before she goes to sleep and being surprised to see the designs painted all over the room. It's fun to comment on the different colors and patterns that you see. In general, the more involved you, the teacher, are in a story the more engaged your students will be. When the teacher "pretends" along with them, they can more deeply enter the world of their imaginations. You may find yourself having fun, too!

VARIATIONS
Instead of telling students which body parts to dip into the paint, ask them to call out suggestions for the group, or individually decide, without speaking, which body parts to use. This challenges the students' imaginations and provides the teacher with an excellent opportunity to assess her or his students' body awareness.

Ask students to visualize the color of their paint before putting their hands in the can. They do not need to name the color out loud, they can simply see it in their minds. Then encourage your students to "see" the color of their designs as they paint the room.

COMMENTARY
This story includes movements which are very important to a child's motor development. Be sure to let the elves spend plenty of time painting on the floor with their tummies because slithering on the floor (technically called "crawling") is a movement they need to experience often. In child development, crawling precedes "creeping" (moving on hands and knees) and walking upright. Research shows that practicing such fundamental movements can be helpful in strengthening neurological pathways in the brain, leading to enhanced perceptual, motor, and cognitive skills. (For a further discussion of developmental movement, see the chapter "Why Movement?")

Another important type of movement for children to experience is cross-lateral movement, in which body parts cross the midline of the body. An excellent example of this is swinging the arms from side to side, as the elves do in swinging the paint can. This type of movement helps children integrate the right and left sides of their brains and is believed to facilitate reading readiness by encouraging the eyes to scan from side to side.

Hopping, as when the elves hop with one foot stuck in the paint can, is an important locomotor movement which requires balance and a sense of one's center of gravity. It is also a precursor to more complex locomotor skills, such as skipping.

Lifting each child at the end of the story is a fun way for the teacher to give each student a moment of individual attention. But do it carefully, remembering to bend your knees and keep the child close to your center of gravity. Teachers with back problems can simply tap each child on the shoulder, signaling them to jump out of the glue.

EXTENSION

This story could lead to a visual art experience, with each child drawing or painting what they think the room looked like after the elves had done their work.

After telling this story, show your students some reproductions of abstract paintings and see if they can identify straight, curved, and zigzag lines in each painting. Then ask them to create their own abstract design using one type of line (i.e., a drawing with only straight lines), or a design combining all three types of lines.

•

KIDS IN TOYLAND

by Pamela Gerke

MOVEMENT CONCEPTS
Speed: Slow, Medium, Fast
Energy: Smooth, Sharp

RELATED ACADEMIC CONCEPT
Social Studies (multicultural holidays)

INTRODUCTION
In this story you will be moving at different speeds. Speed means how fast or slow you're going. Wiggle your fingers slowly. Now wiggle your fingers quickly! Now show me a speed that's in between: Wiggle your fingers at a medium speed.

This story also has movements that are smooth and sharp. When birds fly through the air, their movements are smooth. Smooth movement keeps going and going, without any stops. Stretch your arms out at your sides and pretend you're flying like a bird. Feel how smoothly you glide on the air currents, your wings lifting and swooping, moving without stops.

Now try sharp movements. Sharp movements have a lot of sudden stops. Pretend you're a woodpecker, a bird that pecks trees with it's beak in order to eat the little bugs in the tree bark. It pecks with sharp, jabbing movements of it's pointed beak, making little stops between each peck..

•

(Children begin by standing or sitting on the floor.)

This is the story of some kids who are visiting their aunt (or uncle). Their aunt owns a toy store and she lives on the second floor of the building, right above the store.

It's night time now, and the aunt tucks the kids into bed.
"Good night!" *(Pantomime tucking them in, turning off the lights and leaving.)*

When she's gone, the kids get up very quietly and slowly tiptoe down a secret passageway that leads to the toy store. They are so excited, they tiptoe faster and faster until they arrive at the store.
As they enter the store, the first thing they see are some brightly colored boxes.
Inside each box is a jack-in-the-box who crouches down, waiting until someone says the magic poem that will open the lid. *(Children crouch down, as if inside a box.)*

Jack-in-the-box,
So quiet and still,
Will you jump up quickly?
"Yes, I will!"
(Children jump up on the last line. They can say the last line with you.)

The kids are delighted and push the clown back into the box and close the lid.
(Children crouch down as before.)

Jack-in-the-box,
So quiet and still,
Will you float out slowly?
"Yes, I will!"

They try it one more time:

Jack-in-the-box,
So quiet and still,
Will you pop up rapidly?
"Yes, I will!"

Now the kids look around the toy store and see some dreidels. Does anyone know what a dreidel is?

A dreidel is a kind of spinning top that Jewish kids play with at Hanukkah time. Some dreidels are made out of clay. They begin spinning slowly and then spin faster and faster until they fall down.

(The following can either be spoken as a chant or sung—see "Dreidel Song," included. The chant or song should begin at a slow tempo which gradually speeds up. The spinning of the children will match the tempo changes. At the end of the song they fall down on the floor.)

Dreidel, dreidel, dreidel,
I made it out of clay,
And when it's dry and ready,
Oh dreidel I will play!

The kids are so thrilled with the dreidels that in their enthusiasm they jump up and down a few times. They try the dreidels again. This time, they pick dreidels with soft, rounded edges that move smoothly.
(Repeat song/chant in a smooth or legato style, gradually increasing tempo.)

Then they notice some dreidels that are broken. These ones spin sharply, with jagged little stops.
(Repeat song/chant in a jagged, disjointed style, making a lot of little stops.)

After playing with the dreidels the kids lay down on top of some big, soft teddy bears. While they rest, the kids look up at all the wonderful mobiles hanging from the ceiling. What do the mobiles look like? *(Children can say what they imagine.)*

Now the kids see some robots in the toystore. These robots are each set on a stand so that they can move in place, but they can't move around the room.

Show me a robot that has the controls turned off and is standing frozen in place.
When I turn the switch on your robot, it will move it's arms up and down.
(Pantomime turning a switch on each child.)
A robot is made of metal and plastic and makes sharp, jagged movements, with lots of stops.
The robots turn their heads from side to side, sharply.
They move their arms up and down sharply.
They bend their knees sharply, like they're marching in place.
Now the robots turn off their own switches and freeze.

Just then, the kids hear their aunt coming! Hide!
(Teacher pantomimes being their aunt or uncle coming into the toystore.)

"I thought I heard some noise down here…Hmm…I guess it was just those pesky mice."
(Teacher pantomimes leaving the store.)

That was a close one! Now, the kids find some toy gliders, a kind of airplane that has no engine and which flies really quietly and smoothly.

The gliders slowly circle around the room.
Then the gliders pick up speed and fly a little faster, swooping and gliding back and forth across the toystore.
Then the gliders slow down, make a gentle landing and stop.

Someone turned on a music box and the kids danced around the store, moving like their favorite toy. Which was your favorite toy in the toystore? The jack-in-the box? The dreidels? The robots? The gliders?
(Music begins. Allow time for free dance, with each child moving like their own favorite toy. Music ends.)

Just then, the kids hear footsteps! *(Teacher makes stomping noise with feet.)*
The kids quickly tiptoe through the secret passageway, back to their bedroom.
When they arrive, they slip into bed and pretend to be asleep.
(Teacher pantomimes entering as their aunt or uncle.)

"Looks like the kids are all right. That's odd—I could have sworn I heard something moving around the toy store!" *(Teacher pantomimes leaving.)*

The kids giggle as they lay in their beds and remember all the fun they had in the toy store.
(End of story.)

MUSICAL SELECTIONS

Smooth, gliding music, such as harp or violin music:

Hap Palmer, "Kite Song," *Pretend*

Eric Chapelle, "Adagio for Two Violins," *Music for Creative Dance: Contrast and Continuum, Volume I*

SUGGESTIONS FOR PRESENTATION

While playing the role of the aunt or uncle, you may also need to model the movements of the children and toys in the story. Be sure to make it clear that gliders are silent ariplanes and do not make loud engine sounds (nor do they have machine guns mounted on them!)

The "Dreidel Song" can either be spoken as a chant or sung (music is included), either with or without instrumental accompaniment. Start the song/chant at a slow tempo (speed) and gradually increase the tempo. The children will respond by increasing the speed of their spinning. Make sure they don't spin so much that they get dizzy. Jumping up and down a little bit between each spin is included to help keep them from getting dizzy. There should be plenty of space between the children so that they don't bump into each other.

VARIATIONS

You can incorporate many other movement concepts into the movements of the toys that the children encounter. For example, instead of having the jack-in-the-boxes jump at different Speeds, they could jump with different Weights (jump strongly or jump lightly.). The dreidels could be of differing Sizes so that the children spin in shapes that are Big, Small or Medium-sized. The gliders could move in different Pathways—Straight, Curved or Zigzag.

This story can be expanded upon to incorporate other concepts. For example, if you want to use the concept of Weight, the kids could find balloons with which they do a Light dance. Halfway through the dance, the balloons could suddenly harden and become giant, heavy marbles which the kids must use Strong muscles to lift. Your students might enjoy using real balloons (blown up prior to telling the story) as a prop for this dance.

It's possible to invent a "secret passageway" to the toy store with the furniture in your room. This will delight your students, as well as help you involve other concepts in the story. For instance, you can work with the concept of Relationships by setting up a creative passageway in which the children must go over a chair, under a table, through a doorway and around a rug. When they exit the toy store, they must reverse the path. Say these prepositions aloud as they travel the passageway. You could invent another passageway based on the concept of Pathways, which requires the children to travel in straight lines, around curves, zigzagging between objects, and so on.

When the story is over, you can sit in a circle and ask each child to share which toy in the store was their favorite, and what they liked about it. Be sure to have children describe their feelings about moving as that toy. For example, did moving as the robot make them feel powerful? In control? Did moving as the glider make them feel gentle? It is important for children to be able to verbalize their feelings about movement.

COMMENTARY

Most children love to spin. Research has shown that spinning is good for children's development, and children are often attracted to movement that helps develop their brains and bodies. Spinning aids with neurological development, including the vestibular system, which helps in maintaining equilibrium. The children may want to spin so much that they get dizzy, so make sure they don't overdo it.

EXTENSIONS

This story can be part of an exploration of different winter holiday traditions. For example: singing and dancing to the " Dreidel Song" is appropriate at Hanukkah time. The toy store could become "Santa's Workshop" with music from Tchaikovsky's "Nutcracker Suite" played for the free dance period. Perhaps the kids might discover corn dolls and dance to African music to celebrate the African-American holiday Kwanzaa, which begins December 26.

DREIDEL SONG

THE PICKLE WHO TOOK A TRIP

by Helen Landalf

MOVEMENT CONCEPTS
> Levels: High, Middle, Low
> Relationships: Over, Under, Around, Through

RELATED ACADEMIC SUBJECT
> Language Arts (prepositions)

INTRODUCTION
> The story I'm about to tell you will make you move on three different levels: high, middle, and low. Show me a low shape that's very close to the ground.
> Show me a high shape that reaches for the sky.
> Now try a middle-level shape that's not too low, not too high.
> Our story today will also make us move with different relationships: over, under, around, and through.

•

(Have children begin standing in a scattered formation in the room. Music begins.)

Once upon a time, there was a pickle who decided to take a trip. It packed its suitcase and started off. The pickle was so happy that it bounced along the road.

After a short time, the pickle came to a cave. Being a very curious pickle, it decided to explore. It crouched over on a middle level, feeling the walls of the cave with its hands as it walked.

The cave turned into a low tunnel and the pickle had to crawl on its hands and knees to get through.

The tunnel became even lower and the pickle had to slither through on its tummy.

At the end of the tunnel was a tiny hole, just big enough for the pickle to squeeze through. Then it began to roll and roll until…BOOM! It bumped into something soft and squishy. The pickle stuck its hand into the soft, squishy thing.
Then it stuck its foot in.
Then its head.
Then it broke off a little piece and tasted it. It was a giant marshmallow!

The pickle stood on tiptoe and saw that it was in a field of giant marshmallows that stretched as far as its eyes could see. So the pickle began to leap… hop… skip… and jump over the giant marshmallows.

(Give children twenty to thirty seconds here to explore high level movements.)

After all that leaping and jumping, the pickle began to feel tired, so it lay down on the ground to take a short nap. But just as it was about to fall asleep…

…the pickle looked up and saw that the giant marshmallows were starting to float away. So the pickle shouted "Hey, wait for me!" Would you like to say that? *(Repeat "Hey, wait for me!" with the children joining in.)*

The pickle jumped up and grabbed onto one of the giant marshmallows. Together they floated forward… backward… sideways… round and round in circles…

…until they came down for a landing in Slitherland, where snakes and other slimy creatures live. The pickle got right down on the ground and began to roll… slither… squirm… wriggle… and writhe with the snakes.

(Give children twenty to thirty seconds to explore low level movements.)

Suddenly, all the snakes slithered into little holes in the ground, and out floated some tiny bubbles. The pickle had to tiptoe very carefully all around the bubbles so they wouldn't pop. But all of a sudden…

Pop! Pop! Pop! The bubbles started popping the pickle into the air! Pop! Pop! Pop!

(You may want to demonstrate doing quick little jumps into the air. Give the children twenty to thirty seconds to explore sharp jumping movements.)

When all the bubbles had popped, the giant marshmallow started to float away again but the pickle shouted, "Hey, wait for me!"

One last time the pickle and the marshmallow floated forward… backward… sideways… round and round…until they were right above the pickle's house.

When the pickle saw its very own house down below, it let go of the giant marshmallow and gently melted to the ground. It rolled up the stairs and straight into bed where it fell fast asleep.

And that is the story of the pickle who took a trip.
(Music ends. End of story.)

MUSICAL SUGGESTIONS

There are three possible ways to provide music for this story. One is to have perky, upbeat music playing in the background through the entire story:

Shadowfax, "Another Country," *Dreams of Children*

Claude Bolling,"Baroque and Blue," *Bolling's Greatest Hits*

The second possibility is to play musical selections only during key points in the story.
1. When the pickle hops, skips and jumps over the giant marshmallows—fast, bubbly:

Eric Chappelle,"Caribbean Leaps," *Music for Creative Dance: Contrast and Continuum, Volume II*

Phyllis Weikert, "Happy Feet," *Rhythmically Movin' 1*
2. When the pickle is in Slitherland—slow, lower-pitched:

Jean Michael Jarre, *Oxygene*

Eric Chappelle, "Whales," *Music for Creative Dance: Contrast and Continuum, Volume II*
3. When the bubbles pop the pickle into the air, you can return to the first selection, or try something unusual, like electronic music or playing beats on a drum.

Yet another way to provide music for this story is to play high and low tones on a piano or other instrument to correspond with high and low movements in the story. The best times to do this would be:

1. High tones for going over the giant marshmallows
2. Low tones for moving in Slitherland
3. High tones or quick ascending glissandos for being popped into the air by the bubbles
4. Descending scale when the pickle melts to the ground

SUGGESTIONS FOR PRESENTATION

Pausing for twenty to thirty seconds in the three key places noted in the script (and above, under "Musical Suggestions") will give children time to explore moving at low and high levels. The verbs listed at these points in the story (leap, hop, skip, roll, slither, and so on) should be considered suggestions for movement rather than specific directions. Your students may choose to do these movements as you name them or create movements of their own. Either response should be accepted and encouraged.

Taking note of some of the creative movements you see and describe them aloud, i.e., "I see Johnny turning in the air as he leaps over the marshmallows! I see Susan slithering on her back!" will encourage your students to experiment with new ways of moving.

VARIATIONS

If you wish to focus more specifically on the concept of Relationships, you can ask students to repeat a relationship word (preposition) over and over as they do it with their bodies. For example, as the pickles are going through the tunnel they could say, "Through! Through!" or "Over! Over!" each time they leap over a giant marshmallow. You can model this by saying the word yourself as your students do the movement, then inviting them to say it aloud with you.

COMMENTARY

As has been mentioned in other sections of this book, experiences of moving on a low level are vitally important for child development (see chapter, "Why Movement Stories?"). Be sure to allow students plenty of time to explore low level movements in Slitherland.

This story is excellent for helping children develop spatial awareness because it requires them to move in relationship to imaginary objects (the cave, the marshmallows, the bubbles). It helps them develop a physical understanding of prepositions which will become important as they begin to read.

You may find that young students moving on a low level tend to cluster together. This is natural. The more they practice moving with others, the more defined their sense of personal space will become.

EXTENSIONS

This story could be the springboard for a music lesson. After discussing ways that the pickle moves on high levels (jumping, leaping, hopping, skipping, being "popped" into the air) and low levels (slithering, rolling, squirming, wriggling, writhing), students could respond with these movements upon hearing high and low tones played on the piano or other instrument. You might even discuss how the pickle moved from high to low when it melted to the ground, and guide your students to feel how this corresponds to a descending scale.

•

ASTRONAUTS IN OUTER SPACE

by Pamela Gerke

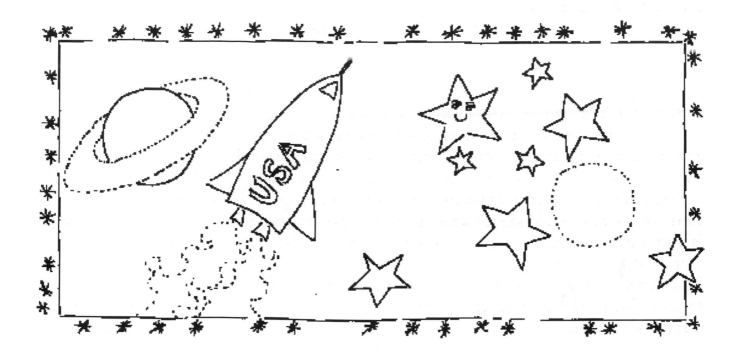

MOVEMENT CONCEPTS
Weight: Strong, Light
Direction: Forward, Backward, Sideways, Up, Down

RELATED ACADEMIC CONCEPT
Science (gravity)

INTRODUCTION
This story takes place in outer space and uses the concept of Weight. What is weight?

In movement, weight tells you how you're using your muscles—either strongly or lightly. First pretend you are strong and are picking up very heavy weights, like an athlete in training. Notice how strong and hard your muscles feel when you pick up something heavy. Put down the weights and pretend to pick up a feather. Feel how soft and relaxed your muscles are when you're lifting something light.

In this story, we'll also be traveling in different Directions. Let's all face this way, (demonstrate which direction to face, such as toward a certain wall in your room) and stay facing that way as we change directions.

Walk forward…Stomp backwards.
Tiptoe to one side…Slide to the other side.
Fall down…Jump up.

(Begin with children standing scattered about the room, in self-space.)

Welcome, fellow astronauts! This is your commander speaking! Today we will take a trip through outer space to the planet XOGO!
But first, we must do our exercises:

Stretch up…Stretch down…Stretch to the side…Stretch to the other side.
10 Jumping Jacks: 1-2-3-4-5-6-7-8-9-10!

Now we're ready. Everyone put on your space suits!
The zipper starts at the bottom and zips up: **ZZZZZZIP!**
There's a zipper on each leg which starts at the top and zips down: **ZZZIP! ZZZIP!**

Put on your space helmets! Now climb the ladder to the spaceship—up, up, up.
Find your seat—for takeoff, we have to lie on our backs and hug our knees to our chests.
Strap on your seat belts!

Countdown: 10, 9, 8, 7, 6, 5, 4, 3, 2, 1, **BLASTOFF!!!**
(Sound effects, while jiggling in place.)

Now the seat belt sign goes off and we can unstrap our seat belts.
Since we're in outer space, there's no gravity to hold us down and we can float lightly and freely around the spaceship!

We float forward…backward…
We float sideways…then to the other side…
We float down, down, down, and roll around on the floor…
We float up, up, up, until we're practically touching the ceiling!

Suddenly, the seat belt warning sign goes on: **BEEP! BEEP! BEEP!**
A meteor shower is headed toward the space ship! Quickly, get back in your seats and strap on your seat belts!

Here comes the meteor shower! **KKKKKK!!!** *(Sound effects, while jiggling in place.)*

The meteor shower has passed—Phew!
Look out the window—we can see our destination planet, XOGO! What color is XOGO?
(Children can say what they imagine.)

Hold on, we're coming in for a landing! *(Sound effects, while jiggling in place.)*
THUD!!! We made it! Now we can unstrap our seat belts.

The air is not the same here as on Earth, so when we go outside we'll have to wear special breathing helmets. Take off your space helmets and put on your special oxygen helmets. Let's go!

Oh, no, the door is jammed shut! It must have been hit by the meteor shower!
We'll have to push with all our strength to get it open!
All together now: **1-2-3-PUSH!!!**
It didn't open—it's really jammed tight!
Let's try again, using more muscles: **1-2-3-PUSH!!!**
It still won't open! We'll have to use all the strength we've got! **1-2-3-PUSH!!!**
We did it!
Now that we're outside we realize that XOGO has a lot more gravity than earth and it pulls our bodies down, down, down. It takes all our strength just to walk! It feels like there are heavy weights on our arms and hands. Are you strong enough to lift up your hands?

It feels like there are weights on our feet and legs. Can you pick up your feet?
Even our heads feel very, very heavy.

Wait—I just remembered: I have some antigravity powder in my pocket! I'll sprinkle it on everyone! *(Pantomime sprinkling powder on all the children.)*

That's better—now we can walk lightly!
Uh, oh! I accidentally used the double-dosage powder!
Now we're so light, we're floating!

(Music begins.)

Let's do a floating dance!

(Allow time for a "light," free dance. After a minute or so, say:)

Now the antigravity powder is wearing off! The gravity of XOGO is pulling us down, down, down, and it takes all our strength to move! Can you still dance when you're so heavy?

(Allow more time for "heavy," free dance. You may want to switch your musical selection here to "heavier" or lower-pitched music. Music ends.)

Look at that—we danced all the way to the space lab!
Inside, the gravity is like earth's and we can walk around normally.

Now it's time to rest. Let's ask the computer for directions to our beds in the space lab.
(Pantomime tapping a computer keyboard.)

The directions say:
First, go forward 10 steps: 1-2-3-4-5-6-7-8-9-10.
Now, walk sideways for 5 steps: 1-2-3-4-5.
Now, walk backward for 8 steps: 1-2-3-4-5-6-7-8.
Forward for 3 steps: 1-2-3.

And there are our beds! Let's lie down and rest now. But wait—there's one last message for us on the computer. It says: "Welcome to XOGO, Earthlings!"
(End of story.)

MUSICAL SUGGESTION

"Space" music, or synthesized sounds. Can use 2 selections:
"Light", floating music:
Jean Jarre, *Oxygene*
"Strong" or "heavy," lower-pitched music:
Grieg, "In the Hall of the Mountain King," *Peer Gynt*
Hap Palmer, "Big, Heavy Box," *Pretend*

SUGGESTIONS FOR PRESENTATION

Have fun with sound effects, using either your voice or percussion instruments for the sounds of the blastoff, meteor shower and landing. The children will relish making the sound effects also.

You can set up part of your room to be the inside of the spaceship, using whatever furniture you have—such as enclosing your rug area with a row of chairs. Being in an enclosed space is a delicious feeling for children and together you can pretend to look out the windows of the spaceship and imagine all that you see.

Don't be concerned if young children do not distinguish right from left as long as they move sideways. "Directions" are distinguished by which part of the body is leading—the front of our bodies leads our movement forward; the back of our bodies leads us backward; the side of our bodies leads us when we move sideways.

VARIATIONS

This story is in the "science fiction" genre, so anything goes with regard to what the astronauts encounter in outer space. You can select other movement concepts to work with and vary the story accordingly. For example, you may want to emphasize the concept of Speed. Perhaps the atmosphere of XOGO has a weird element that makes everyone move very slowly. Then a windstorm sweeps through which alters the chemistry of the air and causes everything to move swiftly.

You can always combine concepts as well. Perhaps you would like to work with both Size and Weight. The astronauts, while floating in the zero-gravity of outer space, encounter mysterious forces that make them all shrink in size. They now move lightly while being small—that is, their body parts are pulled close to the center of their bodies. When the astronauts arrive on XOGO they encounter the heavy gravitational forces of the planet and must now move with strength while still being small. They then meet a native of XOGO who reverses the forces which had previously shrunk them and now the astronauts grow to become monstrously huge—their body parts extend away from the center of their bodies—so that they move strongly while being big in size.

COMMENTARY

There are several places in this story that involve counting. Numbers, counting, and beginning mathematics can be taught effectively with movement activities.

EXTENSION

Set up an art project to follow, such as having the children invent and draw their own maps of XOGO or draw pictures of the native XOGOites. The group can create the interior of their space ship with tables and chairs and decorate cardboard boxes for the ship's instrument panels.

This story can be integrated with a science activity that teaches about gravity, or perhaps a science project on the importance of air for life on earth (such as growing seeds with and without an air supply). Another possible related activity is a unit on the planets or outer space.

The imaginations of your space-age and computer-age children will be fired up by the setting of this story. This story provides an opportunity for your class to dream of other planets and future possibilities. Your class might create a science fiction book of drawings of their invented planets, with written descriptions of these creations (either dictated to the teacher or written by themselves).

•

THE MONKEY AND THE DOTS

by Helen Landalf
inspired by an idea by Anne Green Gilbert

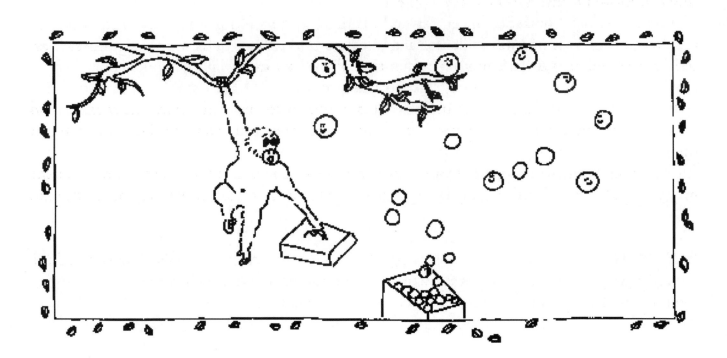

MOVEMENT CONCEPT
    Focus: Single, Multiple

RELATED ACADEMIC SUBJECT
    Learning Skills (concentration)

INTRODUCTION
    Let's do a story that uses the idea of Focus. Focus tells us how we use our eyes when we move. When we use single focus, we look at just one thing at a time. Let's try it:
    Focus on the ceiling
    Focus on the floor
    Focus on your elbow
    Focus on me!
    Multifocus is when we let our eyes wander all around. Let's try that for a moment, standing right where we are.

•

(Have children begin standing in a scattered formation.)

This is the story of a monkey who lived in the jungle. The monkey loved swinging from tree to tree.

(Move through the room reaching hands overhead cross-laterally—crossing from one side of the body to the other—as if grabbing onto tree branches.)

One day, as the monkey was swinging along it looked down and saw something unusual on the floor of the jungle. So it jumped down to take a closer look.

There, right in the middle of the jungle, was a big silver box with a lid on it. The monkey had never seen a box before, so it tiptoed carefully around the box, trying to figure out what it was.
The monkey decided to open the box to see what was inside. The lid was very heavy, so the monkey had to use all its muscles to get it open. Let's count to three, then try to lift the lid. One, two, three, lift!

(Children will usually all cluster around one imaginary box instead of finding their own. This is fine, since it allows them the group experience of trying to lift the lid together.)

But the lid wouldn't open. So the monkey tried again. One, two, three, lift!

The lid *still* wouldn't open, so the monkey tried one more time. One, two, three, LIFT!

This time the lid popped open and the monkey stared into the box. It was full of little dots! Red dots! Blue dots! Green dots! Purple dots! The monkey reached into the box and put one dot into its hand.

(Music begins.)

The monkey moved its hand around slowly, staring at the dot.
Then, suddenly, the dot jumped off the monkey's hand and landed on its foot. The monkey began to hop along, staring at the dot on its foot.

Then the dot jumped off the monkey's foot and landed on its elbow. The monkey began to slide sideways, looking right at the dot on its elbow.

Next, that crazy dot jumped right onto the monkey's back. The monkey twisted and turned, trying to see the dot on its back.

Oh my goodness! The dot jumped off the monkey's back and began flying through the air, all around the jungle. The monkey chased it—over here! No, over here! No, over here! No, over here!

Finally the monkey jumped into the air and grabbed the dot.

But when the monkey opened its hand, there were not one, but two dots inside! The monkey juggled the two dots, just like a circus juggler. *(You may need to model juggling the dots.)*

The monkey looked up to see that all the dots were jumping out of the box. There were hundreds of colored dots flying through the air! The monkey began to dance: spinning… leaping… jumping… and rolling as it tried to see all of the dots.

The monkey heard a noise. "Oh dear, someone is coming. I'd better put all these dots back in the box." So the monkey carefully picked all the dots out of the air… off the trees… off the ground… and put them back in the box where they belonged.

The monkey closed the lid with a BANG and went swinging away through the trees. Then the monkey curled up in a tree and fell fast asleep.

(Curl into ball on the floor. Music ends. End of story.)

MUSICAL SUGGESTIONS

Lively, humorous:

Hap Palmer, "Tipsy," *Movin'*

Hap Palmer, "Changes," *Getting to Know Myself*

SUGGESTIONS FOR PRESENTATION

As an introduction to this story, you may want to show your students some "sticky dots" or have them use dots in an art project before telling the story.

It is possible to tell this story with children remaining in a seated position, either in a circle on the floor or at desks. They can open an imaginary box right in front of them, see the dots on various body parts, and pull imaginary dots out of the air. To tell the story in this way, simply omit the locomotor actions (hopping, leaping, turning, and so forth) and emphasize the use of the students' eyes, heads, and upper bodies.

It is helpful for the teacher to convey a sense of excitement in his or her voice to facilitate the strength of the children's focus. Modulating the pitch (sometimes speaking in a high voice, sometimes low), volume, and tempo of your speaking voice will add a sense of theatricality to your storytelling. This is a dramatic skill which requires practice but which will be rewarded by your ability to pull your students deeply into a story.

COMMENTARY

The Movement Concept that this story emphasizes—Focus—is a useful one to introduce and practice. Single focus, putting all of one's visual attention on one thing, is strongly related to concentration, putting all of one's mental attention on one thing. For example, you may notice in telling this story that your students seem particularly quiet and concentrated when the monkey is tiptoeing around the box. This is because they are shutting out distractions in their effort to put their visual attention on one thing—the box. In so doing, they are also focusing their mental attention. You can remind students, at other times during the day when you wish them to concentrate, of how they felt when they were the monkey tiptoeing around the box and putting all of their attention on one thing.

The movements required of children in this story are helpful in developing eye tracking, a prerequisite for reading. Sustaining focus on an imaginary object (a dot) and following that object as it moves through space is just as beneficial in strengthening tracking ability as following the movement of a real object. (An example of "tracking" a real object is watching the movement of a penlight during a visual exam.)

Reaching cross-laterally, as the monkey does when it swings from tree to tree at the beginning of the story, is another movement helpful in developing reading readiness. Reaching across the midline of the body helps integrate the right and left halves of the brain and encourages the eyes to scan from side to side. (For further discussion of cross-laterality, see the chapter, "Why Movement?" For suggestions on how to teach cross-lateral movement, see the Movement Skills Glossary.)

VARIATIONS

This story adapts well to seasonal variations. Around Halloween time, replace the word "dots" in the story with "ghosts," "bats," or "spiders." In winter they can be colored snowflakes. In spring you can choose to have the box be full of butterflies. You will doubtless discover other variations, based on the interests of the children in your group.

EXTENSIONS

After telling the story, your students interest in "dots" will be high, so you might want to use dots for some other classroom activities. You could count or sort colored dots as a math activity, or do a dot-to-dot visual art project.

•

CREATING YOUR OWN MOVEMENT STORIES

Perhaps, after using the movement stories in this book, you would like to try creating a few of your own. Great! Here are a few pointers to get you started on that process:

A good Movement Story will:
1. Clearly center on a movement concept or concepts
2. Encourage a variety of movements
3. Be open-ended enough to allow for movement exploration and experimentation
4. Be structured enough to keep children focused and engaged
5. Appeal to a child's sense of imagination, adventure, and humor

Begin by choosing a concept from the Movement Concept chart (see Chapter 2) that you would like your story to emphasize. Your completed story may end up encompassing more than one concept, but it's best to start with just one.

Next, brainstorm activities or situations where that concept would be put into action. Think of as many ideas as you can—you can always narrow your choices later. It might also be helpful to look at the list of loco-motor and nonlocomotor movements to locate movements that seem to fit with your concept.

For example, your brainstorm list for the concept Weight (strong, light) might look like this:
lifting a heavy object
a rock
something hidden under a rock
light floating snowflakes
a snowstorm
pulling on a rope
balloons floating
weight lifter
popcorn popping
ghost
elephants walking
tiptoeing lightly—don't wake a baby
stomping strongly—angry

As you can see, it would be difficult to incorporate all of these elements into one story. So now it's time to pick a few that might fit together and that suggest a situation to you. Looking at the above list, I can imagine an elephant who is searching for a hidden treasure and has to lift many heavy objects to find it. Perhaps the elephant gets caught in a snowstorm, with snowflakes floating lightly all around. And when the elephant opens the heavy lid of a treasure chest—out float some balloons!

Your next step will be to choose a main character or characters for your story. Using an animal or inanimate object as your main character helps circumvent the issue of whether the character is male or female. While children have no trouble identifying with a talking cat or a leaping pickle, little boys may have great resistance to doing a story about a princess and girls may have difficulty identifying with a story about a little boy. Fantasy characters such as elves or dragons can be fun, but be careful about using images that are too frightening for your students.

Once you have chosen a Movement Concept, a main character, a situation, and have a list of movement words you'd like to incorporate, you are ready to build your story. Your story may be very logical and sequential or surreal and dreamlike. It may be serious or silly. Use your intuition, experiment, and be open to changing your ideas. Be sure to include sections in your story where the children can dance freely, as well as sections where their movements are directed.

To review, here are the steps for creating your own Movement Story:
1. Choose a movement concept or concepts
2. Brainstorm images, activities, and situations related to that concept
3. Choose a main character or characters
4. Build your story

If creating your own story from scratch feels a bit overwhelming, start small by varying one of the stories in this book. Tell the same story, but emphasize a different movement concept. Change the ending of a story, or create a new main character. Gradually your confidence in your creative abilities will grow and you'll find yourself creating stories on your own.

It is also possible to create Movement Stories collaboratively with the children in your class or group. One way of accomplishing this is to sit down with the children before their movement session and brainstorm ideas together, following the steps above. Children are usually highly creative, divergent thinkers, but may need your guidance to put the events of the story into a logical sequence. After you have created your story verbally, have the class immediately get up and try it in movement.

If you are not afraid of a little chaos, it's also possible to create a story with children spontaneously, while they are moving. Start with a familiar situation and character and ask them to call out suggestions for varying it as you tell the story. For example, if you were using the story "The Pickle Who Took a Trip," you would start by saying, "Once there was a pickle who decided to take a trip. So it packed its suitcase and started off. The first thing the pickle came to was a...." Allow the children to call out ideas or ask them to raise their hands if they have an idea to contribute. The most difficult task here is choosing which idea to use! Continue this way through the story, adding variations as you go. This method requires spontaneity and flexibility on the teacher's part, but the students will be proud to have created their own story. You can later put the story into written form and ask your students to illustrate it.

Last of all, keep your senses open for all the story ideas that are just waiting to be discovered. You can learn to see the spark of a story in a leaf blowing on a windy day, the sound of a rainstorm, or the feel of hot pavement beneath your feet. Sometimes a story may come to you as you relax in a hot bath, work in your garden, or in those fertile moments just before sleep. Or perhaps it will be just a word or a thought from the mind of a child that becomes the seed of your next Movement Story.

GLOSSARY

CRAWLING—slithering on the belly

CREEPING—moving on hands and knees

CROSS-LATERAL—movements that cross the midline or center of the body, such as swinging the arms from side to side

GALLOPING—sliding forward with one leg always in front of the other. To teach, say to the children: "One foot is the leader and the other foot chases it." It's also helpful to have them pat the thigh of their forward leg with one hand to remind them which leg stays in front.

HATHA YOGA—a science of asanas, or postures, designed to facilitate the development of self-awareness, bodily and mental control, and well-being

HOMOLATERAL—only one side of the body moves at a time

KINESTHETIC—referring to physical sensations experienced by the body through touch or movement

LABAN MOVEMENT ANALYSIS—a system of describing, notating and analyzing movement, as developed by Rudolph von Laban. Born in the late 1800s, Laban did most of his work in movement analysis in the 1930s and 1940s and died in 1958.

LOCOMOTOR—referring to traveling movement—movement that transports the body from one place to another in space, such as walking, running, and so on

MULTIPLE INTELLIGENCES THEORY—Developed by Howard Gardner, this theory identifies seven different types of intelligence: linguistic, logical-mathematical, musical, visual-spatial, bodily-kinesthetic, interpersonal, and intrapersonal. Gardner believes that all humans possess all seven intelligences and that the different strengths and combinations of these distinguish one individual from another. Interdisciplinary teaching, such as that found in arts education, enhances learning by stimulating and utilizing all types of intelligence.

NON-LOCOMOTOR—referring to movement that is stationary—movement that does not transport the body from one place to another in space, such as bending from side to side

SKIPPING—Children master this skill independently when they are ready, usually around age 4–6. The tricky part for beginners is alternating legs. To teach, demonstrate skipping while alternately tapping each knee as it lifts, saying, "Knee, knee," and so on. To give extra help, stand facing a child and hold their hands while they skip forward and you skip backward, asking them to copy or "mirror" you.

VESTIBULAR SYSTEM—one of three systems that helps us to know where we are in space (the others being vision and proprioception—knowing where one part of the body is in relation to the rest). The vestibular system consists of a semicircular canal with several loops, located in each inner ear. These canals are lined with tiny hairs and are partially filled with a gelatinous fluid that is sloshed or disturbed every time the body moves. This fluid is drawn toward the earth by the pull of gravity so that, depending on where our heads are oriented at the time, those hairs nearest to the ground are stimulated more that those that are farther away from it. This helps us to sense our relationship to the earth.

DISCOGRAPHY

Bolling, *Claude, Bolling's Greatest Hits*

Brewer, Rumble, and Tingstad, *Emerald*

Chappelle, Eric, *Music for Creative Dance: Contrast and Continuum, Volumes I and II*

Debussy, *Suite from Peleas and Melisande*

Deuter, *Call of the Unknown*

Galway, James, *Annie's Song*

Grieg, *Peer Gynt*

Jarre, Jean Michel, *Oxygene*

John, Esther Little Dove, *The Elements, Volume II*

Palmer, Hap, *Getting to Know Myself*

Palmer, Hap, *Movin'*

Palmer, Hap, *Pretend*

Palmer, Hap, *Seagulls*

Pica Rae, *Move and Learn*

Shadowfax, *Dreams of Children*

For information on ordering Eric Chappelle's *Music for Creative Dance: Contrast and Continuum, Volumes I and II* write or call:

Ravenna Ventures, Inc.
4756 University Village Pl. N.E. #117
Seattle, WA. 98105
(206) 528-7556

BIBLIOGRAPHY

BOOKS ON MOVEMENT AND THE BRAIN:

Ayres, Jean A., Ph.D. 1972. *Sensory Integration and Learning Disorders,* Western Psychological Services.

Delacato, Carl H. 1977. *A New Start for the Child with Reading Problems.* New York: Macmillian

Gardner, Howard. 1983. *Frames of Mind: the Theory of Multiple Intelligences.* New York: New York University Press.

Lewinn, Dr. Edward D. 1977. *Human Neurological Organization.* Springfield, Ill.: Charles C. Thomas Publishers.

FOR FURTHER INFORMATION ON MOVEMENT AND THE BRAIN, WRITE TO:

Bette Lamont, Director
Developmental Movement Center
10303 Meridian Ave. N. Suite 201
P.O. Box 75681
Seattle, WA. 98125

BOOKS ON THE WORK OF RUDOLPH VON LABAN:

Bartenieff, Irmgaard, with Lewis, Dori. 1980. *Body Movement: Coping With the Environment.* New York: Gordon and Breach Science Publishers.

Laban, Rudolph von. 1963. *Modern Educational Dance,* Second Edition. London: MacDonald and Evans.

FOR FURTHER INFORMATION ON THE WORK OF RUDOLPH VON LABAN, WRITE:

Laban-Bartenieff Institute for Movement Studies
11 East 4th Street 3rd Floor
New York, NY 10003

BOOKS ON TEACHING CREATIVE MOVEMENT AND DANCE:

Carr, Rachel. 1973. *Be a Frog, a Bird, or a Tree.* New York: Doubleday and Co. (Yoga for children)

Canner, Norma. 1975. *...and a time to dance.* Boston, MA: Beacon Press.

Gilbert, Anne Green. 1992. *Creative Dance for All Ages.* Reston, Virginia: American Alliance for Health, Physical Education, Recreation and Dance.

Gilbert, Anne Green. 1977. *Teaching the Three R's Through Movement Experiences.* Minneapolis, Minn.: Burgess Publishing Company.

Joyce, Mary. 1994. *First Steps in Teaching Creative Dance to Children,* Third Edition. Mountain View, CA: Mayfield Publishing Company.

Morningstar, Moira.1986. *Growing With Dance.* Heriot Bay, B.C.: Windborne Publications.

FOR MORE INFORMATION ON DANCE EDUCATION, WRITE:

National Dance Association
1900 Association Drive
Reston, VA. 22091
(703) 476-3436

ABOUT THE AUTHORS

Helen Landalf has been choreographing, performing, and teaching dance in the Seattle area since 1987. Her solo choreography has been showcased in several Seattle venues. She has choreographed four pieces for Kaleidoscope Dance Company, a modern dance company of young people. Helen is on the faculty of the Creative Dance Center and is an Artist in Residence for the Montana Public Schools. She frequently presents workshops for classroom teachers on integrating dance into basic curriculum.

Pamela Gerke is author of *Multicultural Plays for Children, Grades K–6* (in 2 volumes), published by Smith & Kraus, Inc. She has been Director and Playwright for Kids Action Theater Play Productions in Seattle since she founded it in 1988 and has written, directed, and produced over twenty-five children's plays, as well as being composer and music director for several other shows. Pamela has worked as a children's music and movement specialist for over ten years and currently divides her time between Kids Action Theater, choral conducting, and composing.

ABOUT THE COVER ARTIST

Mark Rimland was one of the autistic savants with whom Dustin Hoffman worked in preparation for his role as an autistic savant in the Academy Award winning film *Rain Man*.

Mark's paintings have been exhibited and have won awards in exhibitions for handicapped artists throughout the United States.

Mark is the older brother of author Helen Landalf